WHO WILL SAVE OUR CHILDREN?

WHO WILL SAVE OUR CHILDREN?

30 Strategies for Protecting Your Child from a Threatening World

COMPILED BY

Beverly LaHaye

Wolgemuth & Hyatt, Publishers, Inc.
Brentwood, Tennessee

The mission of Wolgemuth & Hyatt, Publishers, Inc. is to publish and distribute books that lead individuals toward:

- A personal faith in the one true God: Father, Son, and Holy Spirit;

- A lifestyle of practical discipleship; and

- A worldview that is consistent with the historic, Christian faith.

Moreover, the Company endeavors to accomplish this mission at a reasonable profit and in a manner which glorifies God and serves His Kingdom.

Wolgemuth & Hyatt, Publishers, Inc.
1749 Mallory Lane, Suite 110
Brentwood, Tennessee 37027

Library of Congress Cataloging-in-Publication Data

LaHaye, Beverly.
    Who will save our children? : 30 strategies for protecting your child from a threatening world / Beverly LaHaye.—1st ed.
        p. cm.
    Includes index.
    ISBN 0-943497-12-4
    1. Family—United States—Religious life. 2. United States—Moral conditions. 3. United States—Politics and government—1989–
4. Education (Christian theology) 5. Sex—Religious aspects—Christianity. 6. Right to life—United States. 7. Conservatism—United States. 8. Conservatism—Religious aspects—Christianity.
I. Title.
BV4526.2.L27   1990
248.8'45—dc20   90-48205
                                                CIP

When this book, *Who Will Save Our Children?*, became more than a dream, it was necessary to find a committed, dedicated person to pull it all together. For that reason I respectfully dedicate this book to Barrie Lyons, who not only assisted on this project but was also one of the founding members of Concerned Women for America and served on the National Board of Directors for many years.

Presently she fills the position of director of Publications and Research. Any influence that Concerned Women for America will have on the future children of America will certainly be shared by Barrie Lyons because of her commitment in using the printed page to educate millions of people.

CONTENTS

INTRODUCTION

M any of our fellow citizens think we are living in a time of peace, for even the Cold War has abated. However, a real and present enemy is within our midst, one infinitely more dangerous to American ideals than uniformed Viet Cong or even Hitler's elite S.S. troops. The tragedy is that we are engaged in a civil war in which conservatives try to preserve our traditional American values, while liberal humanists seek to destroy them.

The future of the coming generation is at stake. Truly, as we approach the year 2000, we have entered a *decade of destiny for our children*. We must unite for action, rally our troops, and plan our strategy to win complete victory over insidious forces of evil that threaten our very existence.

We must make our stand on seven fronts, which will go down in history as important as the battles of Kings Mountain or Iwo Jima:

1. The battle for the babies. The future of America depends on our return to the sanctity of human life. From state to state we must begin working at organizing rallies, lobbying, activating a legislative strategy in each state to secure the passage of pro-life legislation, and calling together prayer/action chapters to help protect the lives of the preborn.

2. *The battle for children's minds (education).* To ensure that the humanistic indoctrination does not effectively besiege the forty-five million children in public schools, we must fight at the local level. Parents in the community must organize parental groups, initiate public forums, and lobby school boards and state legislatures.

3. *The battle against pornography.* We must organize a public outcry for the prosecution of porn peddlers nationwide; we must write our district attorneys and lobby our legislators to pressure for enforcement of the statutes already enacted. We must also monitor the entertainment industry and write the sponsors of lewd programming.

4. *The war on drugs.* This battle will not be won by an act of Congress nor in legislatures alone; it is one that every citizen must take the responsibility for in his or her own community. Parents must provide their children with values for living and good local church youth programs; they must be on the alert how and with whom their children spend their spare time. Parents should also be community leaders in seeing that the local schools are drug free and have sound drug education programs.

5. *The battle for the legislatures.* We must cause our legislators to represent the majority of people. Citizens must learn to speak out and be heard from their city council to the White House. We need more moral-minded people elected to offices on every level.

6. *The battle to protect our First Amendment rights.* The right to free speech, free press, and free exercise of religion must be protected at every level.

These freedoms do not include purging Biblical truth from our public institutions.

7. The battle in prayer and action. Every success we have had has been based first in prayer and then followed up with action. We must make prayer our first focus, for every victory will be won with prayer. We need women, men, and pastors to stand together, first with prayer, then with action.

This book contains articles that have appeared in the *Concerned Women for America* monthly newsletters. The purpose then was the purpose now: to increase your understanding of the battles we face. Becoming informed is the best preliminary strategy. At the end of each chapter are Focus Points for consideration, to direct your thinking and to help you devise campaign strategies.

Read thoughtfully, pray earnestly, then "be strong in the Lord and in the power of his might. . . . Take up the whole armor of God, that you may be able to withstand in the evil day" (Ephesians 6:10–13).

1

THE SUICIDE OF THE WEST

Albert Veldhuyzen

*To think that we may be living in the twilight of
Western civilization is appalling, but the hard facts
are that we may be entering the end of our age.
Our self-destruction—suicide—is deliberate as op-
posed to annihilation by outside forces—murder.
Can the trend be stopped?*

One of the most frequently used arguments to
justify our modern day abortion holocaust is
the myth of population explosion.

Paul Ehrlich, a prominent neo-Malthusian
doomsdayer, predicts that if the world's population
doubles, mankind will be in danger of extinction by
starvation. He says, "A cancer is an uncontrolled
multiplication of cells; the population explosion is
an uncontrolled multiplication of people. . . . We
must shift our efforts from treatment of the symp-
toms to the cutting out of the cancer. The operation

will demand many apparently brutal and heartless decisions."

Heartlessness becomes a virtue and brutality a commendable trait in the distorted world of humanist utopians. Such fallacious reasoning has legitimized abortion-on-demand and the prevalent secular mentality that having many children is somehow incompatible with social responsibility. The message being presented fits in neatly with the present day idols of our materialistic and pleasure-oriented society. Liberals soothe their consciences and disguise their selfishness by inventing "moral" reasons for abortions and childless families.

The trends show that the secular humanist message has been accepted by most of the industrialized world. Abortions are rampant throughout the West, and nations are already failing to maintain their present populations. In order to reproduce itself, a country needs on average 2.1 children per family. No Western nation today attains that average. The U.S. average has fallen below 2.0, and in West Germany and Denmark the average has dropped to 1.3. If it weren't for immigration, the U.S. population would be decreasing.

The *Chicago Tribune* reported that "Italians may be doomed to extinction if the nation's birthrate continues to plunge." In France the need is considered so acute that posters of chubby-cheeked babies with the headline "France Needs Babies" are being put up. French demographer Pierre Chaunn wrote: "The rejection of [marriage and family] is a recent phenomenon. For the moment it is limited to the sixth of the world that constitutes the developed nations, the eight hundred million men and women who have decided to commit the strangest collective suicide of history."

The myth of starvation has been confirmed by the experience of many Third World nations. The fertility rate is still very high in many countries which are today self-sufficient in food production but fifteen years ago were considered hopelessly unable to provide for themselves.

These myths have been accepted by many, especially within the mainline denominations such as the Episcopal, Presbyterian, and Methodist churches. Commenting on the dwindling numbers of liberal Protestants, *Newsweek* said that "mainliners are having fewer children. Indeed, the Presbyterians [P.C. (U.S.A.)], with a birthrate (1.97) well below the replacement level, seem bent on vanishing like the Shakers."

Martin Luther, one of the fathers of the Protestant Reformation, condemned those "who seem to detest giving birth lest the bearing and rearing of children disturb their leisure." The canonization of the secular humanist mindset of self-indulgence is as old as civilization itself and has resulted in the decay and death of once powerful and prosperous nations.

Bishop Dionysius in ancient Rome lamented the rampant childless marriages and historian Will Durant records that within Roman society "childlessness was spreading as the ideal of a declining vitality. . . . The decay of the ancient faith among the upper classes had washed away the supernatural supports of marriage, fidelity, and parentage; the passage from farm to city had made children less of an asset, more of a liability and a toy; women wished to be sexually rather than maternally beautiful; in general the desire for individual freedom seemed to be running counter to the needs of the race."

When men and societies lose sight of God's dominion mandate of subduing the earth for His glory (Genesis 9:1), they will suffer the consequences. If present trends continue, the choices will be physical extinction or government mandated creation of test-tube babies as wards of the state, resulting in the irrelevance of the family structure, the bedrock of any viable civilization.

If the European peoples and culture are to survive in the third millennium A.D., a drastic change in the mindset of Western man will be necessary. Ideas do indeed have consequences; history has shown only those rooted in Biblical truth provide the basis of a prosperous, compassionate, and flourishing civilization.

FOCUS POINTS

1. Who was Thomas Malthus and what was his economic theory?

2. Why is Paul Ehrlich called a "neo-Malthusian doomsdayer"?

3. Why did the *Chicago Tribune* say the developed nations are committing "the strangest collective suicide in history"?

4. In what five ways can American society today be compared to the decline of the Roman Empire as described by historian Will Durant?

5. What changes are needed to ensure survival of European-based culture in the third millennium A.D.?

6. What can you do to help offset the present trend toward "physical extinction or government mandated creation of test-tube babies as wards of the state"?

2

THE BONDAGE OF ABSOLUTE FREEDOM

It may sound like an oxymoron, but "the bondage of absolute freedom" is no mere figure of speech. It produces real fetters that inspire escape attempts through substance abuse and suicide. How can we build walls that do not a prison make?

A struggle between two competing concepts of freedom enthralls contemporary American society. There exists the Biblical concept espoused by the founders of this great nation which recognizes the responsibility that accompanies freedom, and there abides the destructive concept of absolute freedom, a freedom with no limitations or obligations.

Those who think only in terms of the founders' concept have no basis upon which to question the legitimacy of anyone's quest for freedom. The pursuit of this celebrated ideal provided the impetus for the birth of our nation. Its principles are embodied in our Constitution, our representative form of government.

The mere mention of the founders' idea of freedom invokes cherished thoughts of the Pilgrims at Plymouth Rock, the Declaration of Independence, Patrick Henry's "give me liberty or give me death" oration, and the valiant war against the Redcoats. Undoubtedly, America's historical concept of freedom is synonymous with all that is moral and just.

Unfortunately, contemporary society cannot boast the same admirable applications of the term. In an effort to justify limitless self-indulgence and self-expression, humanists have severed freedom from responsibility and formulated the narcissistic ideal of absolute freedom or complete independence from all authority outside of the individual. Each individual is considered the center of his universe and the sole authority, the very essence of the philosophy of humanism.

Nowhere has this irresponsible egoism been more conspicuous than in our public school system. The crusade for absolute freedom is replacing education in the three Rs with instruction designed to liberate our children from their confining belief in God, the oppressive authority of their parents, and their backward values and beliefs. The irony is that this pursuit of absolute freedom threatens to enslave the very children it is intended to deliver.

What does this quest for deliverance entail? And what are its consequences?

First, the exercise of absolute freedom requires the denial of any higher authority than man. Adherence to a God-ordained value structure logically follows a belief in God. Liberation from an inhibiting structure of absolutes requires rejection of the Absolute Authority. Thus, the "freedom crusaders" in the public schools promote the "science" of evolution and condemn the "religion" of creation. They hush the fact that the evidence overwhelmingly points to the existence of a Creator, and they continue to fraudulently perpetuate evolution as a validated scientific theory. The consequence: children are "liberated" from the tyrannical rule of God—free to pursue their own desires and design their own truths.

But freedom is not what results. Man is made in the image of God and nothing the evolutionists say can negate this truth. Our God-given ability to reason provokes our search for significance. Alienated from God, children cannot find the answers to their oft-asked questions: Who am I? Why am I here? Where am I going? Their lives have no meaning and they feel no inherent worth. They find themselves in the midst of a hopeless struggle for purpose, purpose they will never discover apart from their Creator.

What about the child's parents? Can they not assist their progeny in solving life's mysteries?

America's freedom crusaders have liberated our children from their trust in parents as well. Absolute freedom allows no dependence upon parental guidance. All truths emanate from the individual. Parental authority is obsolete and illegitimate.

In an effort to prove parents' illegitimacy, the crusaders consistently thrust our children into situations in which they must defend the legacy of beliefs passed on to them. Disillusionment with those beliefs results when the child is unable to articulate and defend his legacy against attacks by the instructor and his peers. Consequently, a child's "truth" becomes the majority opinion arrived at in that classroom, on that day. Parents are disregarded because their values were not sanctioned by the class.

But children's estrangement from their avenues of support is not enough for the noble freedom crusaders. The quest for true liberation also entails confronting all of life's complex issues and crafting solutions or responses to each. Thus, our public school classrooms are transformed into psychological playgrounds where children are forced to formulate their beliefs on different issues. This pathetic pilgrimage demands an exhaustive look at death, a graphic look at sex, and an open look at drugs.

Thousands of America's public school children are writing their obituaries in English class, viewing pornographic material in health class, and hammering out independent opinions on the morality of drug abuse during ethics class.

No wonder our children have become obsessed with self-sufficiency and their ability to arrive at truth. Their only means of survival in the Malthusian classrooms of this era is the ability to prove their worth and offer sanctioned solutions. Peer approval becomes their only source of fulfillment and the only indication that they may have stumbled onto the answers for life's puzzling questions.

Where is the freedom, the deliverance, in this disheartening struggle for significance and validity? Bondage, not freedom, is what drives our children to alcohol, drugs, and suicide. Substance abuse and suicide are attempts at escape, not assertions of their newfound liberties.

Individuals require a support structure that can protect, comfort, and yes, provide parameters. Only with the help of that structure and within those boundaries can an individual—child, teenager, or adult—exercise true freedom.

Biblical absolutes are not an index of prohibitions, but an enumeration of what is best for individuals and what will offer them true fulfillment. God loved man enough to give him parameters. Parents must love their children enough to share with them those same boundaries and their foundation.

Likewise, Christians and conservatives must love their children and this country enough to actively oppose attempts to undermine Biblical absolutes. The responsibility to provide and protect God's value structure is not restricted to the confines of one's home. We must directly confront those movements that threaten to wreak havoc on our value structure. Our children's pathetic quest for liberation will cease when parents accept the responsibility to protect and defend the only beliefs and values that offer true freedom.

FOCUS POINTS

1. Look up the word *freedom* in a good dictionary and determine its various meanings.

2. What elements do you think are necessary components of true freedom?

3. How can freedom be destructive?

4. How do some humanists misunderstand what freedom really is?

5. How do children often react when enslaved by absolute freedom?

6. What can parents specifically do to help their children exercise true freedom?

7. Pray for the resurgence of our Western civilization.

3

MORAL INSTRUCTION AFFECTS YOUTH IN EVERY AREA OF LIFE

William J. Bennett

William J. Bennett, former secretary of education under Reagan and now President Bush's general in the war against drugs, is a former classroom teacher. Speaking at the 1988 Concerned Women for America (CWA) convention, he made a plea for moral instruction for today's youth.

S everal people have said to me during the last three years that my work at the department—standing up for a strong curriculum, for basics, for math and history and English and science—was all to the good, and they appreciate it very much.

But some people say, "We wish you had avoided this whole area of values, this whole fuzzy area of values, because that's tricky and because that makes us uneasy."

It was very interesting to me that a lot of my colleagues from higher education, my former university professor friends, used to clap whenever I talked about more math, English, history, and science, but used to wince when I talked about religion and the need for moral instruction and the like. They said, "Don't talk about those will-o-the-wisp things. Talk about the hard things, the real things." Well, the real answer, of course, as you know, is that there is nothing more real than moral considerations. There is nothing more fundamental.

I give you the following story as an example. A friend of mine who is a detective in Washington, D.C., working on narcotics, once gave me a very interesting document. It was a document prepared by a sixteen-year-old young man in the District of Columbia. It was three pages of records on drug deals. The last page was a map of where the drug deals were made and where the people were located, the various guards, the fourteen-year-old with the gun, the car, the pick-up, and the beepers. The other two pages were calculations of sales—percentage of take, how much he had to pay to his supplier, and so on.

As a document in mathematics and design, it deserved an *A*. There were no mistakes—no addition mistakes, no subtraction mistakes—not even any misspellings. Even the map was correct. There was only one thing wrong with this document: it was testimony to the total moral corruption of this young man.

This is a good example of what Richard C. Cabot wrote fifty years ago: "If there is no education of men's purpose, if there is no ethical basis at the foundation of education, then the more we know, the smarter villains and livelier crooks we may be." If that knowledge and that wisdom is not put to the right direction, into the right activities, it hardly will benefit us at all.

Now let's talk a minute about teenage pregnancy. My wife, who has taken it upon herself to go to schools, public and private, to talk to teenagers—girls—about why they should avoid sexual intercourse, has had a number of interesting conversations about this. She started by talking to tenth-grade girls, telling them why they should wait, why it was important to wait, why it was prudent to wait, why it was correct to wait. She received a very good reception from the young women with whom she spoke.

What troubled her, as she told me, was that many of the girls said the following two things: "This is the first time anybody has said this to me," and "You're a little late, Mrs. Bennett. I think you should talk to the sixth-grade girls, not the tenth-grade girls."

My point is this: nature abhors a vacuum, and adolescence abhors a vacuum, too. If we do not speak, it will not mean that others will not speak. If you do not make the case for what you believe, it does not follow that the people of the other point of view will not make theirs. They will make theirs. Again, one cannot simply throw up one's hands. One cannot simply act to remove a curriculum or course of study. One must put something else, something better, in its place.

Young people's notions of themselves, the sense of who they are, what they can be, and what they want to be are the factors that are most powerful in influencing sexual activity. Your sense of who you are, who you can be, and who you want to be is the most powerful influence in determining and predicting sexual activity. That is reality. Who the young woman or who the young man thinks she or he is, what they think is worthy of them in terms of their lives and activities, will most powerfully determine how they behave.

This question of values, this question of right and wrong, is no will-o-the-wisp; it is no extra factor. It is no other thing that perhaps from time to time we should consider. It's the heart of the enterprise because it is those things—values, or if you will, convictions, beliefs, the orientation of one's soul, of one's personality—that will determine conduct. In our age, and this point cannot be made too emphatically, values and beliefs will not just determine conduct but will have an awful lot to do with whether that person is sound in a moral sense and can maintain his health and his well-being in other ways. The epidemic of AIDS hasn't radically changed the rules of the game. It's just given us one more compelling reason to say and to act on what we've always known to be true.

FOCUS POINTS

1. According to Mr. Bennett, one's values determine conduct. Whose responsibility then is it to instill proper values in young people?

2. How does one go about doing this? Be specific.

3. If a child—or group of children—is not receiving a sound, value-laden underpinning

for life, what, if anything, can interested people do?

4. What is your reaction to the statement "You're a little late, Mrs. Bennett. I think you should talk [about pregnancy] to the sixth-grade girls"?

4

CHILDHOOD: A TIME FOR INNOCENCE OR INDOCTRINATION?

Sinister influences permeate seemingly innocuous childhood diversions like toys, games, cartoons, and comics. Responsible parents must be alert to the impact of children's entertainment and take steps to hold the industry accountable.

How should the first sixteen years or so of a child's life be spent? Should it not be primarily a happy, carefree time, innocent of life's possible hazards, sorrows, and defilements? Or should it be a period used to infest a child's mind with his potential for mind power, mystical experiences, and sexual experimentation?

The influence of secular humanism is infiltrating all areas of the entertainment industry for children: books, comics, television programming, movies, games, toys. In the guise of entertainment (they must be entertained lest they become bored), children are being exposed to megadoses of occultic practices, violence, and sensual behavior. Is this a devious design to casually desensitize the future generations to traditional moral values?

Parents need to be alert and aware. If asked, most adults would recall their own childhood as the most carefree time in their lives, that fairy tale period when they did little more than wander from one source of amusement to another: games of hide and seek, Archie and Veronica comic books, Popeye and Roadrunner cartoons, and Hotwheels and hula hoops.

Unfortunately, this nostalgic reminiscence, as pleasurable as it may be for adults, can pose a threat to our children when parents presume that their walk down memory lane is indicative of childhood today. Assuming that a child's journey of amusement is as innocuous as it was twenty to twenty-five years ago has resulted in the unfettered entertainment industry's wreaking havoc on the minds of many children.

For the alert parent, it takes little more than a Saturday breakfast in front of the television to realize that the days of Donald Duck and Popeye have long since past. Some old favorites still exist, but the cocaine-snorting Mighty Mouse is more characteristic of today's cartoon industry than the spinach-eating Popeye.

Violence, drugs, sorcery, wizardry, occult influences, and Egyptian paganism are now standard fare. In fact, Phil Phillips, author of *Turmoil in the Toy Box*, states that over 80 percent of contemporary cartoons deal with the occult. Exercising the power bestowed upon them by their gods or demons, characters cast spells, perform levitation, and practice mind control and astral projection. They employ the "powers" of healing crystals, forces of light, crystal balls, and magical potions.

According to Phillips, the groundbreaker for occult cartoons, "He-Man and the Masters of the Universe," features a character that transforms himself from a wimp into the most powerful force in the universe by praying to a demonic spirit. Skeletor, a villain in the series, carries a ram's head staff, the symbol of demonic power. Another character called Teela sports a cobra collar and carries a cobra staff, a symbol of demonic power and protection. And the "He-Man" series is not alone in its violence and occultism. If in doubt, check the *TV Guide* on Saturday morning.

Spin-off toys from the cartoons allow children to consume themselves in violence and paganism. Marketing strategy involves releasing cartoons and toys at the same time. The cartoons serve as advertisements for the toys and program their audience to play with the toy in a certain manner. For example, children can watch "He-Man" each morning at 6:30 A.M. and then spend their days absorbed in He-Man's world by purchasing the plastic character, his villainous and "heroic" counterparts, and other paraphernalia related to the cartoon series. Mattel has reportedly made over one billion dollars marketing this He-Man series of toys.

Toy manufacturers and retailers are capitalizing on our children's newfound fascination with violence and the occult. Take a look at Mongor, the "slithering evil serpent," and his partner, Ming the Merciless. Figures such as the Supernaturals are packaged to promote the fact that they can "release their hologram powers" to transform themselves from "a wizard to a wise old owl," "a wicked witch to a hissing cat," and "a vampire to a swooping bat." The Nintendo video games feature "Tamboo—The Sixth Sense," the "Legacy of the Wizard," "Friday the 13th—Destroy Jason if you can," and the "Demons of Death."

According to Phillips, the most popular war toys are within the Transformer series. Some of these include Robotech, Voltron, and GoBots. The toys may appear harmless, but the glamorization of violence on the cartoon series should make parents take a second look. At last review, "Transformers" was the most violent cartoon on television. Other violence-promoting toys include the Rambo series, the G.I Joe series that bears little resemblance to the original G.I. Joe, the Power Lords, and the new Teenage Mutant Ninja Turtles.

Another series of "playthings" prominently displayed in the toy stores, perhaps a spin-off of the Garbage Pail Kids, are the Madballs. These mangled and hideous heads have names such as Slobulus, Bash Brain, Skull Face, Swine Sucker, Wolf Breath, Bruise Brother, and Fist Face. Along this same line are toys that spew and ooze disgusting slime and sludge. The Spitballs series, ugly but not quite as offensive as the Madballs, spits water at the unsuspecting chump who gets close enough to inspect the figure.

What about children's games? Hide and seek and kickball no longer appeal to most children, but are we knowledgeable about what replaced them? Fantasy role-playing games are the new craze. Included in this category are Photon, Assassin, the National Survival Game, and the infamous Dungeons and Dragons (D and D). Photon is a sophisticated game of laser tag that allows children and parents alike to dress up in futuristic attire and play out their violent fantasies on an elaborate space-age battlefield. Assassin is a "game" in which participants put contracts out on their opponents, plan their strategy, and then move in for the kill. The National Survival Game is yet another "fun" pastime in which participants dress up in militaristic apparel and shoot opponents with weapons that fire paint pellets.

Most participants would probably dismiss these games as nothing more than innocent attempts at releasing tension, but the impact these games could have on young, impressionable minds cannot be discounted. In fact, according to Bob Maddux, the author of *Fantasy Explosion,* the *Sacramento Union* reported an incident in which a teacher found fifth and sixth grade students engrossed in a role-playing game. However, this game involved posing as drug dealers, using flour for cocaine, oregano as marijuana, and Monopoly money for cash.

Even if one could ignore the impact upon our children and argue the innocuous nature of the previously mentioned games, one role-playing series that merits no justification is Dungeons and Dragons. Within a framework established by the referee or Dungeon Master, children create their own character and then embark on a particular quest. Participants can assume the character of an honorable knight, a low-class thief, a god, or a demon. The quest of their particular character may require that they torture, seduce, rape, cast spells, participate in demon worship, and pray to pagan deities.

According to Phillips's book, one Dungeons and Dragons guidebook states, "Serving a deity is a significant part of D and D, and all player characters should have a patron god."

One of the most destructive aspects of this game, second only to dabbling in the occult, is that players become obsessed with the world of Dungeons. The line between fantasy and reality frequently becomes so blurred that the particular D and D quest becomes some participants' reality.

Equally as disturbing as the changes in our children's playthings are the changes in another source of childhood amusement: the comic book. Contemporary comic books are so savage and decadent that to call them comics is an undeniable misnomer. In fact, psychiatrist Thomas Radecki, chair of the National Coalition on TV Violence, states: "Believe it or not, the comic book rack has become the most violent section of the bookstore." His research indicates that "87 percent of the regular bookstore comics and 95 percent of those sold at specialty shops feature harmful themes of violence."

And if the violence in the comic book is not sufficient, take a look at the advertisements on about every fourth page. They promote the violent Nintendo games and toys such as artificial rocket launchers, mine detectors, body armor, grenade launchers, iron gloves, plastic explosives, and remote control missiles.

John Fulce, the owner of a comic bookstore for eight years and now president of Entertainment Media Awareness, says that contemporary comics now feature seduction, graphic sex, merciless killing, occult themes, witchcraft, homosexuality, prostitution, suicide, and necromancy.

Fulce adds that the heroes in these comics are what one would term *antiheroes*, heroes that will do anything and everything to stop the criminal. One thirteen-year-old described the antiheroes as "people who have gone insane for the good of it." The new Batman is indicative of this perception. He may stop criminals, but the movie's screenwriter, Sam Hamm, told *Citizen* reporter Joseph Farah, "I wrote Batman as a psychotic, this guy who's having a terrible crisis of conscience."

Other antiheroes may not be portrayed as psychotic, but they do drink, smoke cigarettes and marijuana, commit adultery, and curse obsessively. One "hero" is portrayed as an avid reader of *Playboy*.

Commenting on the move toward more "mature" themes, John Davis, a major comic distributor, told *Forbes* magazine, "They [the readers] do like to see the characters sliced and diced." And they must because the comic book industry has doubled to over $300 million in the last decade. A few examples of the new trend of violence and decadence include:

- Marvel's *New Universe* line which features a character who has sex with three women in one issue.

- Marvel's *Alpha Flight* which spotlights a homosexual character dying of AIDS.

- One issue of the DC book *Heebie Geebies* which contains what appears to be a rape scene with the woman finally surrendering.

- DC's *Green Lantern* which contains a scene depicting a woman who teases a man by stripping in front of him.

Comic book publishers justify this trend by asserting that comics are no longer for children. They tell critics that comics other than Archie and Casper are for adults. Yet any child can buy these comics, and some of the most grotesque examples such as the *Terminators*, *The Uncanny X-Men*, and *Justice League Eu-*

rope contain advertisements for Mr. Bubbles sweatshirts and Count Chocula cereal. Is the public to believe that these advertisements are directed at adults?

Clearly, allowing the irresponsible entertainment industry to continue unchecked will result in our children's walk down memory lane more closely resembling a nightmare than a fairy tale.

It is time that parents become more alert to the impact of children's entertainment and take steps to hold the industry accountable. We can no longer assume that toys, games, cartoons, and comics are by their very nature innocuous. Children's sources of amusement are not immune to the decadent evolution occurring throughout the entertainment industry. They are, in fact, a subtly permeating influence in the development of future adults who will become desensitized to not merely the declining moral standards we see today, but to even more bizarre forms of human degradation in future generations, helping to reach the goal of a completely secularized America by the twentieth century.

FOCUS POINTS

1. Have you thoughtfully assessed your child's diversions? Spend time in the next few days watching movies or TV *with* your child, reading *with* him or her, playing *with* the toys and games. Keep a journal of your findings.

2. Talk with your child about why he or she likes—or dislikes—particular cartoons, or toys, or reading material.

3. Go to retail outlets and observe the kinds of offerings available for rental or purchase. Keep a journal of your findings.

4. Discuss your findings with parents of your children's friends.

5. Do you feel the situation warrants action? How can you alert other parents to real and present dangers? What can you and other responsible parents do to combat the dangers?

5

EARLY CHILDHOOD EDUCATION: AN ATTEMPT TO FURTHER SOCIALIZE AMERICA

Threatening the American family and the future of our children is the move to foist upon us full-day programs in the public schools for three- to five-year-olds. Instead, the impressive track record of home schooling is moving testimony of parents' ability to serve as the primary educators of their children.

C avalier attempts to socialize the American family out of purposeful existence have become standard fare in our nation's educational and political circles. The dogmatic social planners advocating these measures ignore credible studies that warn against intervening in familial roles, distort existing research to support their positions, and refuse to confront evidence of the importance of the family unit. They have their own agenda and care not what havoc these measures will wreak on American society.

The vigorous campaign for early childhood education is no exception. The National Education Association (NEA), the National Organization for Women
(NOW), humanists, and many childhood
developmentalists are promoting all-day preschool programs in the public schools for three-, four-, and five-
year-olds—despite the growing body of evidence that
these measures will negatively impact our children.

These groups may employ profamily rhetoric, but
their goals are anything but family oriented. Each of
them has something to gain through state control of
youngsters and plans to see its objectives achieved
regardless of the programs' effects on these most vulnerable Americans.

What do these antifamily contingents hope to
gain? According to an NEA official in Nebraska, the
impetus for their involvement is the jobs these initia-
tives would provide, not a commitment to children.
NOW's desire to raise children equally and liberate
women from the oppression of motherhood moti-
vates them to work for state control. Humanists have
consistently claimed the public schools as their battle-
ground for reshaping children's values. And early
childhood "experts" assume they can cure all the
"social evils" of the day if they gain control of
America's children before parents have the opportunity to ruin them with private economic interests
and/or familial, cultural, and spiritual allegiances.

In the face of voluminous data to the contrary,
these contingents have been successful in legitimiz-
ing preschool programs through what can be justly
described as the exploitation of research. Analytical
results from the infamous Perry Preschool Project in
Ypsilanti, Michigan, which bore little resemblance to

typical preschool programs, are consistently cited as a demonstration of these programs' effectiveness.

According to developmental psychologist Raymond Moore, what the advocates fail to mention is that this project concentrated on disadvantaged children, used a lower pupil-teacher ratio than most programs, had much more federal money than typical programs, employed a well-educated and highly motivated staff with a great deal of continuity, and operated more in the home than is standard in most programs. The results of the project study indicated that the children involved in this compensatory preschool program had half the rate of teenage pregnancy, were half as likely to become dependent on welfare, and had much lower rates of criminal activity and juvenile delinquency than their nonschooled counterparts.

Assuming these results are indicative of what could be expected from similar programs (a point of some controversy), there are definite problems with using a study of this nature to legitimize programs for *all* three- and four-year-olds. First, duplication of the student-pupil ratio, the highly skilled staff, the large federal grants, and the in-home instruction required to obtain those results would be cost prohibitive in statewide programs. Second, one cannot apply the results of programs for the disadvantaged to all children. In fact, even the researchers of the Perry Preschool Project express concern over the use of project results to justify enrolling all preschoolers. Too many studies have shown that children from normal homes fare much better than institutionalized children. The home situation is grave when it cannot surpass the care of an institution.

Another important point to consider is that studies of compensatory preschool programs like Head Start reveal no long-term benefits. Furthermore, not one replicated study of any preschool program proves that preschool is better than care in homes where parents provide warm and sensitive nurturing. Dr. Raymond Moore states, "In review of more than 8,000 studies—no matter which discipline—I have not been able to find a single replicated experiment that has clearly demonstrated the desirability of early schooling or day care for the normal child who by some extra effort can have the security of a *reasonably good home.*"

Most empirical studies indicate that institutionalized preschoolers display more aggressive tendencies, experience failure more often, suffer intellectual burnout, and endure much greater incidence of disease. There is also a tendency for children to interpret the separation from their parents as rejection. This sense of rejection and betrayal, coupled with the more frequent failures experienced by early entrants, inevitably results in lower self-esteem.

David Elkind, president of the National Association for the Education of Young Children, states, "Parents who are concerned about their children's academic success should remember that children's self-esteem is as important as their intelligence in determining whether they achieve in school and in life."

Peer dependency is another serious problem exacerbated by early education programs. In fact, researchers from Cornell discovered that this trait is pervasive among institutionalized preschoolers. Peer dependency occurs when children are not permitted sufficient time with their parents to internalize family values before they are assaulted by the beliefs of their peers. In essence, parents who surrender their children to public school programs are leaving them vulnerable to these persistent assaults. Moreover, it is this vulnerability that the humanists hope to capitalize upon in their attempts to undermine the family unit and teach our children "to believe in human potential, not God."

Much to the chagrin of many child developmentalists, home-schooled children not only demonstrate exceptional confidence in themselves and their principles, but they display excellent academic potential as well. In fact, the home-schooled children of America average in the top 25 percent in achievement, the top third in sociability, and score virtually zero in delinquency. Contrasting these figures with our public schools' steady decline in achievement and consistent escalation in delinquency is condemnation enough of public education, not to mention early entrance.

The impressive track record of home schooling is moving testimony of parents' ability to serve as the primary educators of their children. Dr. John Bowlby, London psychiatrist and director of the World Health Organization on Early Childhood Development, takes that appraisal one step further with respect to early education by insisting that a relatively ineffective home is still better for a child than a reasonably good school.

Educational and political crusades that truly want to offer children the competitive edge must recognize the educational importance of the home environment and reject the arguments of self-serving special interest groups who want to remove children from their secure surroundings too soon.

The education and upbringing of children is the primary responsibility of parents. Selfishly or ignorantly surrendering this role would be a grave disservice to our youth as well as our free society. The family must cling to its God-ordained roles, or future generations will suffer the consequences.

FOCUS POINTS

1. Why do some groups favor state control over very young children?

2. How can they justify this stance?

3. When might their arguments be valid?

4. Under what conditions are these programs not in the best interests of the children?

5. What is the track record for home schooling?

6. Why should concerned parents work together to keep early childhood education in the private sector, rather than as a government agency?

6

FEDERAL CHILD CARE: SOCIALIZATION OF FUTURE GENERATIONS

Kimberly Parker

"Social parenting," ostensibly designed to increase productivity of the labor force by freeing American women of child-care obligations, is in reality a disguised attempt to abet the move toward an atheistic, socialist society. Dedicated mothers must resist the "benign" concept of federal child care and cherish their God-given right to preserve the nuclear family.

From the time of its introduction, the Act for Better Child Care (the ABC bill) became the subject of tremendous debate. Unfortunately, arguments over specific provisions and methods of funding served to cloud the true agenda of many groups supporting the legislation. If the truth be known, for many special interest groups the push for government-regulated child care is not an effort to answer the needs created by an alleged child care crisis, but an attempt to use children as pawns in an artful strategy aimed at destroying the nuclear family and moving America toward a more socialist society.

For the first 180 years of our country's existence, families were responsible for raising the children. Care outside the home was only condoned as a stop-gap measure to solve certain family crises. The 1909 White House Conference on Children summed up public sentiment: "Home life is the highest and finest product of civilization. . . . Except in unusual circumstances, the home should not be broken up for reasons of poverty."

It was not until the 1920s that "professionals" in the field of sociology began to claim that the family was unable to fulfill its responsibility and therefore "experts" would have to step in and assist. The claims by these so-called professionals opened the care of our children to a vast amount of speculation.

In reality, this move was not a reaction to a need but rather the first attempts at taking children away from parents and placing them in an environment conducive to developing independent moral standards and values. The American public began to buy into the seemingly benign arguments of then-prominent social psychologist George Mead who said, "Gender-free, noncompetitive playthings properly presented in a day-care center could produce a new generation of children, trained to be independent in their moral judgement yet cooperative in their social activities."

In 1930, the White House Conference on Children publicly espoused the judgments of Mead and other professionals, issuing the following statement: "If the grouping of little children for a few hours each day for educational activities and for habit-training through nursery schools is found to be desirable in itself, then this service should be extended on behalf of children generally, regardless of the economic status of the family."

Day-care centers sprang up throughout the country, and organizations rushed to provide funding. Day care was no longer viewed as a temporary measure but as a developmental imperative. Credibility for "social parenting" had been established.

The next thirty years witnessed the increase of federal intervention in child care to meet the demands of national emergencies. For instance, World War II initiated an increase in child care when women began joining the labor forces of defense factories.

The end of the war brought an end to any programs that had been established. The role of parenting was returned to the family and the value of motherhood was reestablished. However, the dangerous precedent of "social parenting" had been set, and its establishment would produce devastating consequences.

In the early 1960s, there was another shift in ideas regarding motherhood. Again, "experts" using faulty logic and distorted facts belittled the mother's role in a child's emotional development. The speculation created by these arguments was immediately seized and used by radical feminists. During the late 1960s, feminists altered the subject of child care to make it an issue of "equality."

Feminists claimed that motherhood oppressed women and that true equality would never be reached until women were removed from this responsibility. To remove women from this "oppressive role," the women's liberation movement revived the devastating precedent of "social parenting." They committed themselves to convincing the American public that the government bears the ultimate responsibility for raising the nation's future generations.

At the National Organization for Women's national conference in 1970, the group declared, "Child care must become a political priority," and called for the establishment of a coalition "to exert pressure on the power structure of labor, industry, and government to immediately make available facilities, funds, etc., and to grant tax deductions for quality child care."

Betty Friedan, a prominent leader in the women's liberation movement, used her book, *The Feminine Mystique,* to communicate the idea that women must leave the home and seek a position in the work force to discover their true identity. Friedan argued: "By choosing femininity over the painful growth to full identity, by never achieving the hard-core of self that comes not from fantasy but from mastering reality, these girls are doomed to suffer ultimately that bored, diffused feeling of purposelessness, non-existence, non-involvement with the world that can be called 'anomie', or lack of identity or merely felt as the problem that has no name." Of course, Friedan's solution to work outside the home was not generated out of her care for this "doomed" generation of young girls but was generated out of her desire to break the bonds of the nuclear family.

In 1981, prominent feminist author Vivian Gornick echoed Friedan's sentiments when she wrote: "Being a housewife is an illegitimate profession. . . . [T]he choice to serve and be protected and plan towards being a family-maker is a choice that shouldn't be. The heart of radical feminism is to change that."

Feminism's desire to create a collectivist society that recognizes no individuals and undermines the family unit goes hand in hand with socialism's desire for the abolition of private property and the communalization of the means of production. In the *Communist Manifesto* Marx and Engels wrote: "On what foundation is the present family, the bourgeois family, based? On capital gain, on private gain. In its completely developed form this family exists only among the bourgeoisie. But this state of things finds its complement in the practical absence of the family among the proletarians, and in public prostitution. The bourgeois family will vanish as a matter of course, when its complement vanishes, and both will vanish with the vanishing of capital." (Note: The preoccupation of the ABC bill's drafters with establishing a proletariat society is manifested in the repeated references in the bill to the productivity of the labor force rather than the emotional and physical wellbeing of children.)

The feminist-collectivist references in Marxist literature are numerous and well-known. Marx wrote, "Social progress can be measured with precision by the social position of the female sex." Lenin said, "It is impossible to win the masses for politics, unless we include the women. . . . We must win the millions of working women in city and village for our cause, for our struggle, and in particular, for the communistic transformation of society."

These movements are one and the same, and their disdain for the nuclear family's role in child development and the inculcation of values is readily apparent. Destruction of the family unit is essential if they are to prevent the "poisoning" of children by private economic interest and/or allegiances to God or culture that would interfere with total commitment to the common good.

The only religion espoused by these movements is secular humanism which raises children to believe in human potential, not God. The *Humanist Manifesto* states, "At the present juncture of history, commitment to all humankind is the highest commitment of which we are capable; it transcends the narrow allegiances of church, state, party, class, or race in moving toward a wider vision of human potentiality." In essence, these humanistic movements believe that to allow the family unit to remain intact is to risk moral "indoctrination" by parents.

Enactment of the Act for Better Child Care, or any bill espousing the government's acceptance of the primary responsibility in child care, greatly enhances the move toward a socialist society. The family unit may ultimately be dissolved, making government-regulated centers free to serve as vehicles in the institutional secularization of future generations into their newly created roles as unisex and valueless automatons—ideal members of a proletarian society.

The nation of Sweden now subsists under the atheistic system these proponents of "social parenting" envision for America. Children's rights have been established, and parents no longer have input in the rearing of their progeny. The difference is that Sweden made its decision to implement government-regulated care as an overt move toward socialism. America, on the other hand, may wake one day from its blissful complacency and realize that socialism has slipped through the back door disguised as the benign concept of federal child care.

The time has come to recognize our children for what they are: the future of America. If America as we know it is to continue to exist, the crucial responsibility for instilling morals and values must remain within the *family*. The freedom we enjoy in this nation depends upon our renewed commitment to this God-ordained institution.

FOCUS POINTS

1. What is the hidden agenda behind the introduction of the Act for Better Child Care (ABC bill)?

2. Historically, how did the concept of "social parenting" become established in American culture?

3. What arguments do those in the feminist movement use to promote legislation imposing federal child care?

4. How does federal child care mesh with Marxist-Leninist doctrine?

5. What is the alternative to the socialist system of government-regulated child care?

6. It's been said that a wise gardener prays for a good harvest, then picks up the hoe. How does this maxim apply in this situation?

7

THE FEDERAL CAMEL IS IN THE FAMILY TENT

John Lofton

A new child-care bill has passed the Congress. Do you know the contents of this bill? What does current research show as the effects of early child care? What is the solution to the child-care problem? Conservative freelance writer, John Lofton, gives an in depth look at this dilemma.

The federal camel's nose has, alas, been thrust even more deeply into the child-care tent. During the final days of the 101st Congress, in late 1990, a child-care bill was passed. Although some congressmen have tried to make us believe that they have put their interest in families in the forefront, we need to take a closer look at this new child care legislative package.

To briefly summarize the effects of the new child-care law:

- It establishes two new day-care grant programs, putting Uncle Sam in charge of the nursery.

- It discriminates against certain families—those where the mother stays at home to care for the child—because (using five-year cost estimates) it spends $5.95 billion on working families who use day-care facilities and spends only $700 million (or $.7 billion) on traditional (mother-stays-at-home) families.

  This child-care law falls far short of President Bush's campaign promise to support child-care legislation that would spend a dollar on traditional families for every dollar spent on day-care families.

- The funds available for vouchers to benefit families that want their children in religious day care will be challenged in the courts, if indeed they are made available at all.

- It does not allow states to handle regulations at the state level. Instead, the federal government now imposes forty-five regulations on states.

One such point at issue may well be public school-based day care. It is expected that this topic will be fought at the state and local levels where court decisions made could affect the allocation of federal block grant monies.

The creation of a block grant program under the House and Senate Labor Committees was just what the day-care lobbyists wanted. Potential loopholes in the legislation's language will permit state day-care lobbyists and bureaucrats to divert significant sums to ambiguous programs or so-called "quality enhancing activities."

The overall projected spending on this legislation is no small amount of money. In addition, the income eligibility threshold for slots created by the two Labor Committees' block grant programs is three-fourths of the state median income. This means, for example, that in states like Connecticut, households with annual incomes in excess of thirty thousand dollars will be eligible for assistance. Thus, this smacks of another middle-class entitlement program—the last thing we need when the national government is operating with a debt of more than $200 billion yearly.

The entire congressional debate on the child-care subject too often boiled down to which "delivery system" was best—tax credits or spending programs. The crucial issue of how children are best reared and served was never the focus of this discussion at all.

And, finally, as happened with the 1988 welfare reform package, under pressure from Senate conferees, a House provision phasing out the Dependent Care Tax Credit for high-income taxpayers was stripped from the child-care bill that became law. This creates a perverse situation where high-income taxpayers with day-care expenses will receive day-care tax benefits, while lower and middle-income taxpayers who care for their own children will receive nothing.

ಶಾ ಶಾ ಶಾ

In terms of the big picture, the fact that Congress has passed a multi-billion dollar child care bill—and programs like this always get bigger, never smaller—is a giant step forward for the liberal/humanist child-care lobby whose goal for a long time has been more government control of families, especially children.

In 1971 President Richard Nixon dealt a crushing blow to the advocates of federal child care when he vetoed S.2007 because it contained $2.1 billion worth of so-called "Child Development Programs." Denouncing the "fiscal irresponsibility, administrative unworkability, and family-weakening implications" of this bill, he called it "radical" and "truly a long leap into the dark for the United States Government and the American people."

An outraged Senator Walter Mondale (D-MN), the chief sponsor of this bill's child-care section, called President Nixon's veto a "totally indefensible act." And, Representative John Brademas (D-IN), the chief House sponsor of this section, declared: "President Nixon has shattered the chances for the healthful and stimulating growth of pre-school children."

Those congressmen, just as their counterparts today, have dangerously overlooked some valuable studies on children. Many child-care experts have clearly stated that raising children in day-care centers is neither healthy nor stimulating for young children.

In a September 1970 article in *Redbook* magazine, Dr. Benjamin Spock wrote, in part:

> If a child develops a real dependence on a substitute who takes over most of his care, and if the substitute then leaves him, *the deprivation will be as great as the average child would feel if his mother had died, and will have long-lasting effects. And if he is repeatedly left by a succession of caretakers, he may develop, as a defense against future desertions, a deep reluctance to love anyone else again.* (Emphasis added)

In testimony against the Mondale federal child-care bill, Dr. Dale Meers, a child psychoanalyst affili-ated with the Children's Hospital in Washington, D.C., repudiated his previous "unreserved support" of day care for the very young. After studying many foreign and domestic day-care programs, Dr. Meers declared: "I became increasingly concerned that the use of early day care was fraught with psychiatric dangers that are as sever as those of the latch-key child of the streets."

In an article in the February 10, 1971, *San Francisco Examiner*, Dr. Edward F. Zigler, head of the Federal Department of Health, Education, and Welfare's Office of Child Development, said that he was "very apprehensive" about setting up what he called "a network of warehouses for children." He called this concept "quite alien to the American ethos."

The *New York Times Magazine* published an article on December 12, 1971, titled, "The Search for the Truth About Day Care." The writer, Sheila Cole, after visiting day care centers in New Haven, Connecticut, and in Moscow, USSR, wrote: "What I found was that most experts in the field of child development think that the ideal place for the pre-school child is home—with mother."

In her book, *The Coming Parent Revolution*, Jeane Westin—who speaks as a "permissive mother who became increasingly guilty, angry, and frustrated while trying to follow the advice of child-rearing 'experts' "—writes:

> Do parents really want day care for their children, or is this just another case of exuberant social engi-neering? Of course, some parents do. But there is evidence that many do not. When Senator Walter

Mondale introduced his Child and Family Services
Act of 1975, which included child care, he received
up to five thousand letters *a day* in protest.

A 1975 study from the University of Michigan
Institute for Social Research found that only 8 percent of five thousand families used professionally-
run child-care centers when they had the opportunity. Most preferred to enlist the help of family
members.

"Permissive mother" Westin adds that while day
care advocates point with pride to European, and
even some Communist, countries for having the fore-
sight to develop child-care programs, both Hungary
and Czechoslovakia eliminated day-care programs
for young children when independent studies con-
vinced officials that such institutional care damaged
pre-school children. And Hungary and Czechoslovakia were, at the time, countries who *wanted* state-in-
doctrinated children!

And this is true today. In fact, today there is even
more information which conclusively demonstrates
the harmful effects of day care outside the home:

- A lengthy article in the September 5, 1984, *Wall
  Street Journal* reports that researchers at the Federal Centers for Disease Control and elsewhere
  are concerned that large licensed day-care centers, which are a home for more than 2 million
  children in the U.S. each day, "are major transmission centers for hepatitis, severe diarrhea, and
  other diseases."

- A November 8, 1984, press release from the
  American Medical Association reports on a study
  in this organization's *Journal* which shows that
  "infants and young children in day-care centers
  contract Hemophilus influenzae type B (the most

common type of meningitis) disease at almost twice the rate as those at home."

- Another long article in the March 3, 1987, *Wall Street Journal* headlined "Day Care for Infants Is Challenged by Research on Psychological Risks," reports that as more working parents entrust their children to day care, some researchers "are warning that day care at too early an age may psychologically harm a child." Jay Belsky, a Pennsylvania State University psychologist who helped forge the academic consensus in the 1970s which claimed that such day care generally benefits a young child, is quoted as saying that his review of ten years of research on day care indicates that such care undermines a child's "sense of trust, of security, of order in the world."

- In a well-documented and thoroughly-researched article in the spring 1988 issue of the Heritage Foundation's *Policy Review*, titled "Brave New World: How Day Care Harms Children," Karl Zinmeister, an adjunct research associate at the American Enterprise Institute, concludes: "While no one has any idea what the ultimate outcome of this giant experiment in proxy child-rearing will be, there is growing evidence that the long-term emotional, intellectual, and cultural effects will be unhappy."

- An article in the April 23, 1988, *Washington Post*, headlined "Study Shows Negative Effects of Full-Time Child Care," reports on a study of primarily middle-class children which was conducted by two female researchers at the University of Texas at Dallas. Their findings: New research indicates that children who are in day care form an early age are more likely to be uncooperative and unpopular by the third grade; such care was also associated with poorer study skills, lower grades, and diminished self-esteem.

- Two articles in the April 1989 issue of the *American Journal of Public Health* report on illnesses that are associated with child-day-care centers. One article reports on a study which shows that children in day-care centers were 4.5 times more likely to be hospitalized than those in other settings. The mean monthly cost of medical care was $32.94 for children in the highest risk settings (day-care centers with the most children in a room); the mean monthly medical cost for children in other settings was $19.78. The second article reports on recurrent outbreaks of gastrointestinal infections among children in a day care center in suburban Dane County in Wisconsin.

In mid-1989 the Federal Food and Drug Administration's *Consumer* magazine featured an article that further substantiates the health and infections risk for day-care children.

So much for Representative John Brademas' absurd contention that a massive federal child-care program would result in "the healthful and stimulating growth of pre-school children."

There is another problem that is at least as serious, maybe more so, than the health and psychological risks to children in day-care centers. This problem is reflected in the file of newspaper stories I have which detail how for years children have been sexually abused, and in some instances killed, in settings licensed and regulated by the state.

This is a key issue because implicit in the demands of those calling for a greater state role in day care is the claim—sometimes made explicitly—that such increased state intervention would, necessarily, result in children that are better cared for.

But this is sheer superstition. Such a claim reveals nothing more than the ignorance of the claimant or his ideological, anti-religious, or anti-traditional family bias—or all three.

Here is just one example of the state's incompetence in the day care area, though I could provide many and have a file full of them: In early August 1984 in New York City, several top officials of the city's child protection agency resigned. They were accused by Mayor Ed Koch of moving too slowly in investigating child abuse cases which led to the deaths of nine children in Brooklyn. A cause of their resignation was the revelation that as many as thirty young children were sexually abused at a Human Resources Administration—administered Bronx daycare center.

ﻻ ﻻ ﻻ

What then is the solution to the day-care problem for those families who do need help in this area? What is the answer if it isn't—as it most definitely is not—more state involvement in the form of direct subsidies, tax credits, or vouchers?

Well, the answer is one that a lot of folks—particularly in Washington, D.C., in the Congress, as well as many across the country—will not like. It involves true self-government and personal responsibility.

First, we need to recognize that government at all levels—federal, state, and local—is trying to do the impossible, which is to play God. They are trying to provide everything for everybody. The result: massive chaos, moral and economic breakdown, huge debt, and a steady reduction in the value of our money and what it buys.

Too many governments and too many Americans are living way beyond their means. One consequence: parents cannot pay their bills. Either one and sometimes both parents work at several jobs. Strangers are then asked to raise their children.

If this is to stop, as it must, government at all levels must drastically reduce what it says it is doing for us. This would mean less debt and a sounder currency with real buying power. And this would mean more workers with more money that was worth something. And most important, a mother could be free to stay at home with her children.

The necessity of living within their means, however, and getting free of any long-term crushing personal debt, would also mandate for millions of families a new lifestyle in which true sacrifice —for their children—would have to occur. This would entail something, quite frankly, that a lot of people may reject—accepting possibly a lower standard of living.

However unpopular, this is the answer—the only answer—to the child-care problem. We must once again take control of our own lives and the lives of our children. The state must not—indeed cannot—be responsible for raising our children. We dare not continue to put the future of our children at risk; the end results are too costly for them and for their parents!

A footnote—indeed a sad one—to the recent federal child-care bill is that among its strongest advocates stood one of our formerly pro-family, traditional values person, Senator Orrin Hatch (R-UT). Both his constituents and friends in Washington, D.C., remember well the position he took when he ran for the Senate in 1977. He actively attacked "the

Washington establishment" and vowed to stand on principle to fight the "growing oppressive bureaucracy." One of his campaign ads promised "a change away from big government and the ever-increasing domination of our lives by the federal bureaucracy."

Many who had always looked to him for leadership in the pro-family issues were shocked to find him standing on the other side of the child-care legislation. In an exclusive interview, never before published, Senator Hatch told me that "with regard to what happened in the early 70s (regarding federal child-care legislation), I still feel that way"—that there should be no such federal role as proposed then. But he says times have changed and what he recently favored is different. "The federal government is the main player in child care already," he said, and now he "thinks only the federal government in this particular case can resolve these problems. They are the only ones who can raise revenue."

This, alas, tells us a lot about why the conservative, pro-traditional family forces aren't doing as well in Washington, D.C., as they should be doing. Too many of our trusted leaders end up saddling the camel and directing his nose under the family tent!

ᴣᴀ ᴣᴀ ᴣᴀ

Let's look at the basic facts simply stated. Listed here, in order of their costs, are some of the main provisions of this new child care law:

1. **Earned Income Tax Credit (EITC).** The cost is $12.4 billion over five years. This will benefit families whose annual income is approximately twenty-two thousand dollars

or less. This refundable tax credit goes to both families who use day care and those who do not.

2. **Child Health Insurance Credit** (introduced by Senator Bentsen). The five-year cost is $5.2 billion. It contains the same eligibility criteria as the EITC and helps poor families offset health insurance costs.

3. **Day Care Block Grant.** An estimate of the five-year cost is $4.45 billion, 60 percent of which must be used for child-care services or to build the child care infrastructure and bureaucracy. States are likely to build the bureaucracy with these funds; otherwise, they may face church-state court battles. There are also coalitions in the states, organized by the Children's Defense Fund, that will lobby heavily for these monies. Twenty-five percent of the funds are reserved for improvement programs for latchkey children, child development, and day care.

States that decide to use the funds for child-care services must make vouchers available to parents who may choose to use the vouchers in religious day-care centers. (During floor debate on this aspect of the bill, Senator Dodd (D-CT) stated that the bill's intent is to allow religious organizations to show preference in hiring and serving members of their faith. This may, however, be challenged in the courts.) The practice of vouchers going to religious child-care providers in itself may very well be challenged in the courts.

4. **Family Support Title IV Grant.** The total five-year cost is $1.5 billion. This grant provides for the child care of working families at risk of becoming dependent on Aid to Families with Dependent Children (AFDC).

5. **The "Wee Tots" Supplemental Tax Credit.** The total five-year cost is $700 million. Eligible families must choose between this credit or the Dependent Care Tax Credit (DCTC), which goes only to day care families. The major portion of the wee tots credit—available to families where the child is under one year of age—will go to families where the mother stays at home with her infant. However, the proportion of funds allotted to daycare families is more than 3.5 times as much as is given to families where the mother does not work outside the home.

6. **Standards and Training Grant.** An estimated five-year cost is $250 million. States will use this money to create standards for child care (facilities, programs, teachers, etc.) and to train and police the child-care providers.

FOCUS POINTS

1. What are the possible areas in which daycare centers can be a harmful environment for children?

2. Can you explain the present child-care legislation in your own words to a friend?

3. What practical changes in lifestyle could you suggest so that child care for the young would be unnecessary?

8

IS HUMANISM A RELIGION?

Dr. Samuel I. Blumenfeld

The cloud of humanism in our public schools is so threatening that I want to share this timely series of articles with my readers. It fully explains exactly what humanism is so there can be no doubts or questions. The author, Dr. Samuel L. Blumenfeld, is a well-known educator with experience in both public and private schools. "Is Humanism a Religion?" first appeared in The Blumenfeld Education Letter, #35, July 1989. Read it and weep. Then dry your tears, be glad you have been given this important information in such cogent form, and start to develop your strategy to protect your child.

The question is important. For humanism is the world view of our educational leaders, of the textbooks they write, of the psychologists who counsel our youngsters on values, sex, and death. In short, it is the world view of the curricula used in the public schools. In fact, humanism forms the philosophical basis of what passes for teacher education in our state colleges and universities.

Establishments of Religion

Thus, if humanism is indeed a religion, then what we have in our public schools and state colleges and universities is government-supported establishments of religion, which is patently unconstitutional and, therefore, illegal.

In fact, it should be pointed out that on March 4, 1987, U.S. District Judge W. Brevard Hand, in *Smith* v. *Board of School Commissioners of Mobile County, Alabama,* ruled that secular humanism is a religion. The 172-page ruling defines religion and concludes, after reviewing the relevant aspects of humanism, that "For purposes of the First Amendment, secular humanism is a religious belief system, entitled to the protections of, and subject to the prohibitions of, the religion clauses."

Three Key Documents

Judge Hand wrote:

> The entire body of thought has three key documents that furnish the text upon which the belief system rests as a platform: *Humanist Manifesto I, Humanist Manifesto II,* and the *Secular Humanist Declaration.*
>
> These factors . . . demonstrate the *institutional* character of secular humanism. They are evidence that this belief system is similar to groups traditionally afforded protection by the First Amendment religion clauses.

The judge then went on to demonstrate that forty-four textbooks being used in the public schools of Alabama were written from the humanist point of view and thereby constituted an illegal establishment of religion. The judge ordered the books removed from the schools.

On August 26, 1987, the 11th Circuit Court reversed Judge Hand's order banning the forty-four textbooks. The higher court did not address the question of whether secular humanism is a religion for First Amendment purposes, but asserted that it was not being promoted in the textbooks that were banned.

Judge Frank M. Johnson, Jr. wrote:

> Use of the challenged textbooks has the primary effect of conveying information that is essentially neutral in its religious content to the school children who utilize the books; none of these books convey a message of government approval of secular humanism. . . .
>
> There simply is nothing in the record to indicate that omission of certain facts regarding religion from these textbooks of itself constituted an advancement of secular humanism or an active hostility towards theistic religion.

And so the books were put back in the schools.

The Wrong Question

But the question is not whether the textbooks are humanistic or not, but whether the entire government education system is an establishment of the humanist religion. All of the rationales used to remove Bibles and other indications and manifestations of the Judeo-Christian theistic worldview from classrooms are based on the First Amendment's prohibition against government establishment of religion.

But if it can be shown that the entire government system of education—from the elementary schools to the state colleges and universities—is an establishment of the humanist religion, the courts would have no choice but to order the closing down of these institutions.

There can be no government establishment of religion in the United States.

Nonsectarianism to Secularism

When the public schools were first established, the courts ruled that the schools had to be nonsectarian, that is, not favoring any particular Protestant denomination. That they were essentially Protestant in character was generally acknowledged. In fact, Catholics established their own parochial school system because they recognized the Protestant character of the public schools.

After the turn of the century, however, as humanist progressives took control of the government schools, nonsectarianism gradually gave way to secularism. Secularists hold that any government institution that promotes or supports belief in the existence of a supernatural being is an establishment of religion.

As more and more judges adopted the secularist point of view, order after order was handed down stripping the public schools of the vestiges of nonsectarian Christianity. Curricula were revised, new textbooks written, new programs instituted so that today's public schools not only no longer reflect the nation's Judeo-Christian heritage, but now constitute the most powerful educational machine for the propagation of humanism among the American people.

Filling the Vacuum

The secularists had no intention of creating a neutral, nontheistic vacuum in our schools. Their plan always was to get rid of Judeo-Christian values and replace them with their own. In this way, the government schools have become, beyond a shadow of a doubt, establishments of the humanist religion.

Today, humanist beliefs are inculcated through such programs and concepts as values clarification, sensitivity training, situational ethics, evolution, multiculturalism, globalism, transcendental meditation, sex education, death education, etc. All of these programs are marbleized throughout the curriculum in reading, language arts, math, social studies, health education, psychology, art, biology, and other subjects. It is impossible for a student in a government school to avoid or escape the all-pervasive influence of humanist ideas and beliefs which confront and accost him daily every which way he turns.

That the plan of the humanists was to supplant traditional theistic religion with a new man-centered religion of their own can be proven by simply quoting the humanists themselves. The best source of these quotes is *The Humanist* magazine.

The forerunner of *The Humanist* was *The New Humanist* which first appeared in 1928 as a monthly bulletin of the Humanist Fellowship, an organization formed by Unitarian students from the University of Chicago and its related theological schools. Its early editors—Harold Buschman, Edwin H. Wilson, and Raymond B. Bragg—were young Unitarian ministers.

It was on the initiative of Bragg that the drafting of *A Humanist Manifesto* (1933) was begun. Professor Roy Wood Sellars wrote the first draft, and the Manifesto appeared in the April 1933 issue of *The New Humanist*.

The manifesto was more than just an affirmation of the humanist world view, it was also a declaration of war against orthodox, traditional religion. The Manifesto's views toward religion can be summed up as follows:

1. The purpose of man's life is "the complete realization of human personality." "[T]he quest for the good life is . . . the central task for man."

2. The humanist's religious emotions are expressed in "social passion," in a "heightened sense of personal life, and in a cooperative effort to promote social well-being."

3. Humanists believe that "all associations and institutions exist for the fulfillment of human life." Therefore, "the intelligent evaluation, transformation, control, and direction of such associations and institutions . . . is the purpose and program of humanism."

In other words, the humanist must take over society's associations and institutions in order to transform them into instruments of humanist purpose. This includes the institutions of traditional religion.

The Manifesto states: "Certainly religious institutions, their ritualistic forms, ecclesiastical methods, and communal activities must be reconstituted as rapidly as experience allows, in order to function effectively in the modern world."

A Messianic Mission

In other words, the messianic mission of the humanists is not to build new institutions of their own, but to subvert and appropriate the institutions of others. This is not a new idea among humanists. The Unitarians subverted Harvard and took it from its Calvinist founders. Religious liberals have appropriated Yale, Princeton, Dartmouth, and other institutions founded by the orthodox.

The loss of these institutions, incidentally, has forced conservative Christians to create new institutions of their own: Bob Jones University, Liberty University, Regent University (formerly CBN University), Pensacola Christian College, and others. The rise of these new institutions has dismayed the humanists who believed that once the major institutions of traditional religion were subverted and taken over, the influence of theistic religion would fade forever. The hopeful demise of traditional theistic religion is a theme frequently expressed by humanist writers.

Humanism as Religion

Roy Wood Sellars, who drafted *Humanist Manifesto I*, wrote in *The Humanist* (Vol. 1, 1941, p. 5) in an article entitled "Humanism as a Religion":

> Undeniably there is something imaginative and daring in bringing together in one phrase two such profoundly symbolic words as *humanism* and *religion*. An intimate union is foreshadowed in which religion will become humanistic and humanism religious. And I believe that such a synthesis is imperative if humanity is ever to achieve a firm and

adequate understanding of itself and its cosmic situation. . . .

To the thoughtful of our day, humanism is being offered as this kind of a religion, a religion akin to science and philosophy and yet not a mere abstract of these specialized endeavors. . . . Religious humanism rests upon the bedrock of a decision that is, in the long run, saner and wiser to face facts than to live in a world of fable.

Humanity as God

An article by Oliver L. Reiser, a signer of the Manifesto, in the same issue of *The Humanist*, states:

The one great hope for democracy lies in the development of a non-supernaturalistic religion which, unlike other intellectual movements, will be non-academic in its appeal to all civilized individuals. This new foundation for a coming world-order must be the emergent outcome of the thought-content of a universalized culture. . . .

The god of this coming world-religion, that is, the object of reverence of scientific humanism, is the spirit of humanity in its upward striving.

Another signer of the Manifesto, William Floyd, wrote in *The Humanist* (Vol. 2, 1942, p. 2):

The religious philosophy of humanism as a substitute for metaphysical theology will enable men to realize the highest value in life without surrendering their minds to any final dogma or any alleged revelation of the supernatural. . . .

To fill the need for a modern conception of religious foundations the *Humanist Manifesto* was issued in 1933.

Another signer, A. Eustace Haydon, wrote in that same issue:

> Like all religions humanism has its world view, techniques and ideal.

In Vol. VI, p. 6 of *The Humanist* (1946), E. Burdette Backus, a Manifesto signer, wrote:

> [Humanism] is indeed a religion, and the extent to which it is capable of eliciting the emotions of men is limited only by a degree in which those who have made it their own shall succeed in embodying its full riches.

Naturalist Religion

In an article entitled "Religion Without God" (*The Humanist*, Vol. VII, 1947, p. 9), Kenneth L. Patton wrote:

> A naturalistic religion is just as inclusive of all that is within the world we know as is the supernaturalistic or theistic religion.
>
> Whereas the theist pins his faith and hope in his God, the humanist and naturalist pins his faith in the natural world, and in man as a creature within it, and his faith is no less magnificent, courageous and hopeful than that of the believer in God.

The Fourth Faith

The 1951 *The Humanist* published an article by Manifesto signer Edwin H. Wilson, entitled "Humanism: The Fourth Faith." He wrote:

> Today, I am suggesting that there is in the world as a present and potent faith, embraced by vast

numbers, yet seldom mentioned—a fourth faith—
namely Humanism. This fourth faith—with rare
exceptions such as some Universalist or Unitarian
churches, a few independent Humanist Fellow-
ships and the Ethical Societies—has no church to
embody it. . . . Theirs is a secular faith.

According to Wilson, the other three faiths are
Protestantism, Catholicism, and Judaism. Since many
of the signers of the Manifesto were Unitarians, it is
not surprising that Wilson identifies the Unitarian
church as belonging to the fourth faith.

In 1952, *The Humanist* (September-October) published an article by Julian Huxley entitled "Evolutionary Humanism: The World's Next Great Religion." Mr. Huxley wrote:

> Out of the needs of our time, through the evolu-
> tionary process, a new religion is rising. By religion
> . . . I mean an organized system of ideas and emo-
> tions which relates man to his destiny, over and
> above the practical affairs of every day, transcend-
> ing the present and the existing systems of law and
> social structure . . . I believe we have nothing to
> lose by using the word "religion" in the broadest
> sense to include nontheistic formulations and sys-
> tems as well.

In the next issue of *The Humanist*, Huxley wrote:

> The next phase of history could, and should, be a
> Humanist phase. Let us help toward its emergence.

Glorification of Man

In an article entitled "The Humanist Faith Today"
(*The Humanist*, Vol. 15, No. 4, 1954, p. 180), we read:

Since humanism appears as a genuinely living option for many people, especially among students, teachers, and intellectuals generally, it may be appropriately studied as a religion. Indeed, it is not unfair to call it the fourth main religious option, along with Judaism, Roman Catholicism, and Protestantism, for thoughtful men in the contemporary Western world. . . .

What remains of religion when the Humanist criticism has completed its work? The Humanist replies that devotion to human and social values emerges as the essence of religion. As [Corliss] Lamont has written, the Humanist postulates that "the chief end of thought and action is to further earthly human interests in behalf of the greater happiness and glory of man."

In 1959, George E. Axtelle, newly elected president of the American Humanist Association, said:

Ours is no revealed religion. It is a religion, an intellectual and moral outlook shaped by the more sensitive and sympathetic souls of our time. . . . Ours is a task, not a doctrine. . . . *Our fundamental goal must be to make the Humanist Way of Life a reality in our communities, our state and our nation.*

In the January-February 1962 issue of *The Humanist*, Sir Julian Huxley wrote an article entitled "The Coming New Religion of Humanism." He wrote:

The beliefs of this religion of evolutionary humanism are not based on revelation in the supernatural sense, but on the revelations that science and learning have given us about man and the universe. A humanist believes with full assurance that man is not alien to nature, but a part of nature, albeit a unique one. . . . His true destiny is to guide the future course of evolution on earth towards greater fulfillment, so as to realize more and higher potentialities. . . .

A humanist religion will have the task of redefining the categories of good and evil in terms of fulfillment and of desirable or undesirable realizations of potentiality, and setting up new targets for its morality to aim at. . . .

Humanism also differs from all supernaturalist religions in centering its long-term aims not on the next world but on this. . . . The humanist goal must therefore be . . . the Fulfillment Society.

Secularists Object

Not all humanists agreed with Huxley. Harry Elmer Barnes and Herbert T. Rosenfeld responded with an article of their own in the July-August 1962 issue. They wrote:

> In our opinion, Sir Julian has set forth not the Humanist ideology of today, but a truly noble and eloquent Unitarian sermon. It is Unitarian doctrine, pure if not simple. . . .
>
> It was, of course, frequently argued in earlier decades of our century that Humanism is a secular religion, but in the light of the history of thought and culture, the terms "religion" and "secular" are, in our view, mutually exclusive. . . . If there is any one thing which characterized and justifies Humanism, it is complete and undeviating secularis. . . .
>
> If Humanism is identical with the latter [Unitarianism] in its ideology, we see little basis for a separate Humanist movement or organization.

Edwin H. Wilson, a Unitarian minister and one of the founders of the humanist movement, responded to the Barnes-Rosenfeld article in the November-December 1962 issue. He told of how the magazine was founded by Unitarian theological students. He went on:

The American Humanist Association itself was organized soon thereafter by a group composed primarily of liberal ministers and professors who were predominantly Unitarians and considered themselves as religious humanists. At the time of its incorporation in 1941, the decision was made not to try to establish humanist churches but to function as an educational movement among humanists wherever they were found.

The early literature of the movement was devoted chiefly to the development of Humanism as a distinctly religious position. . . .

Of the 34 persons who signed the *Humanist Manifesto* in 1933, all but four can be readily identified as "religious humanists" who considered Humanism as the development of a better and truer religion and as the next step ahead for those who sought it. . . .

My conviction is that a probe into what is actually believed would show that the "liberal Unitarian position" and what is generally presented as Humanism—whether as a religion or as a philosophy—differ very little. . . .

One minister who belongs to the A.H.A. said: "We Unitarians in my church have no ideological conflict with the American Humanist Association. Naturalistic Humanism is our position."

Barnes and Rosenfeld question whether a secular religion is possible. Not to make any one word too important, one could argue that today's Unitarian Universalism is a secular religion. . . .

Now for expediency. In the Torcaso case the court recognized Buddhism, Taoism, Ethical Culture and Secular Humanism as religions existing in the United States which do not teach what is traditionally considered belief in God. We should at least ask ourselves whether there are not practical advantages to be had by accepting this decision.

And so, to Wilson, and many other humanists, "secular religion" was not a contradiction in terms. The words defined a nontheistic faith. Comments by readers of the articles appeared in the January-February 1963 issue. Opinion was divided. The hard-core atheists objected to the use of the word "religion," while the Unitarians agreed with Wilson.

Humanist Manifesto II

In 1973 the humanists produced *Humanist Manifesto II,* an affirmation of the earlier document with updated views on the world's social problems. The new Manifesto was as hostile to traditional theistic religion as the earlier one. It said:

> As in 1933, humanists still believe that traditional theism, especially faith in the prayer-hearing God, assumed to love and care for persons, to hear and understand their prayers, and to be able to do something about them, is an unproved and outmoded faith. Salvationism, based on mere affirmation, still appears as harmful, diverting people with false hopes of heaven hereafter. Reasonable minds look to other means for survival. . . .
>
> We believe . . . that traditional dogmatic or authoritarian religions that place revelation, God, ritual, or creed above human needs and experience do a disservice to the human species. . . . We find insufficient evidence for belief in the existence of a supernatural; it is either meaningless or irrelevant to the question of the survival and fulfillment of the human race. As nontheists, we begin with humans not God, nature not deity. . . .

[W]e can discover no divine purpose or providence for the human species. While there is much that we do not know, humans are responsible for what we are or will become. No deity will save us; we must save ourselves.

Ethics and Sex

Manifesto II also spelled out the social and political agendas for humanists:

We affirm that moral values derived their source from human experience. Ethics is *autonomous* and *situational*, needing no theological or ideological sanction. . . . We strive for the good life, here and now. . . .

In the area of sexuality, we believe that intolerant attitudes, often cultivated by orthodox religions and puritanical cultures, unduly repress sexual conduct. The right to birth control, abortion, and divorce should be recognized. . . . Short of harming others or compelling them to do likewise, individuals should be permitted to express their sexual proclivities and pursue their life-styles as they desire.

Humanists also believe that civil liberties must include "a recognition of an individual's right to die with dignity, euthanasia, and the right to suicide."

World Government

The humanists again committed themselves to the goal of World Government. Manifesto II states:

We deplore the division of human-kind on nationalistic grounds. We have reached a turning point in human history where the best option is to *transcend the limits of national sovereignty* and to move toward the building of a world community in which all sectors of the human family can participate. Thus we look to the development of a system of world law and a world order based upon transnational federal government.

Conclusion

Anyone who bothers to study the curriculum of American public education will find in virtually every course and program the tremendous influence of humanist philosophy. It almost seems as if the public schools have become the parochial schools of humanism wherein American youngsters are aggressively indoctrinated in humanist values and ideas.

In fact, humanist editor Joe R. Burnett suggested as much in the November-December 1961 issue of *The Humanist* (p. 347) when arguing in favor of federal aid to education. He said:

> Humanists obviously have a vital interest in the passage of a strong bill for federal aid to public education. Without wanting to push the analogy too far, one might say that public education is the parochial education for scientific humanism.

If that was the case in 1961, it is even more so today. The conclusion is unmistakable: Public education today is a government-supported establishment of the humanist religion.

FOCUS POINTS

If your child attends a public school, you must be ever alert for humanistic tendencies.

1. Have you looked over his or her textbooks?

2. Do you discuss with your child what transpires in class? (Never do this as an inquisitor, but, rather, in a relaxed, quiet time together, as an interested person.)

3. If you discover inappropriate sections in the books or assignments being made, here are some suggested steps to take:

   - Talk to the teacher. Often, when teachers hear your concerns, they will allow your child to be excused from the objectionable activity.

   - Check yourself for bad attitudes. Approach teachers or school officials with a respectful, conciliatory attitude. This does not compromise your Biblical beliefs, but rather confirms your Christian inheritance.

   - Offer an alternative. Try to understand why the teacher has assigned the material. Develop an alternative that meets the teacher's goals but avoids conflict with your beliefs. Explain in a clear, concise, noncondemning way why you find the assignment objectionable and ask that your child be allowed to use your suggested alternative.

   - Appeal to higher authorities if the teacher says no. Follow the same steps as appealing to the teacher. Do not approach school officials with an arrogant or condemning attitude.

   - Consider whether you should home school your children or send them to a Christian private school.

4. Parents must be sure that their children are protected from the ravages and seductions of worldly thinking. They must be diligent to exercise their oversight effectively. How are you trying to do this?

9

EDUCATION IN THE YEAR 2020

Beverly LaHaye

The following is a speech that I made in July 1988 at the Family Forum in Atlanta, which focused on the State As Super Teacher: What Will Our Public Schools Be Teaching in 2020?

In our rapidly changing world of ever-accelerating competition, ever-larger opportunity for personal achievement, and ever-greater demands for success, we can discuss no topic of greater significance than the education of America's future generations.

In discussing our current educational system and its future, I believe it would be helpful to first establish a historical perspective. After all, the progressive education movement, introduced in the 1800s, is largely responsible for the dilemmas we face today.

The first common or public schools were established in New England. Their purpose was two-fold: to promote learning in general and religious study in particular. These schools, established by the Puritan orthodoxy and supported by local communities, were to encourage the furtherance of religious discipline.

Public schools were not conceived to solve a problem of illiteracy. No such problem existed. In fact, literacy was a prerequisite for attending the public grammar schools at age seven; 70 to 100 percent of the population were literate.

Public education was also not provided for in the Constitution. Of the 117 men who signed the Declaration of Independence, the Articles of Confederation, and the Constitution, only one of every three received any formal schooling and only one of every four attended college. Education was viewed as the private responsibility of individual families and communities.

However, in 1805, Harvard University, founded as a seminary for the education of future clergy and magistrates, fell under the control of the Unitarians, extollers of the virtues of moral and religious relativism. It became the fountainhead of the movement toward social reform.

For the misguided Harvard elite, education and the public schools were the means toward eliminating evil. They rejected the Calvinist view that man was innately sinful and blamed ignorance, poverty, and social injustice for the evils of the day—evils that could be eliminated with the right education.

With the fall of Harvard began the militant struggle of our educators for control of the public education system. The Unitarians, or progressives as they were later called, viewed public education as the vehicle toward cultural and social reform, reform that would eliminate moral absolutes. Traditional educators, however, viewed education—public or private—as the development of intellectual skills in combination with moral instruction based upon Judeo-Christian values.

Despite the eloquent arguments of the traditionalists, the American public was seduced into acceptance of the progressive movement by the promise of social improvement and the hope of discovering freedom from what many believed to be the theological tyranny of Calvinist thought.

Traditionalists continued to have an impact on the curriculum taught in America's schools, but the drift toward a truly secular and humanist educational system had begun.

Today, after more than one hundred years of public education and billions of wasted taxpayer dollars, it is immediately apparent that our system of education has evolved into the morally relativistic reform movement envisioned by the progressives.

In 1910, only 2 percent of the American public was classified as illiterate—twenty-two out of every one thousand. Today, the United States spends approximately $282 billion each year on education, yet there are 23 million functionally illiterate adults.

About 13 percent of all seventeen-year-olds in the United States can be considered functionally illiterate. Functional illiteracy among minority youth may run as high as 40 percent.

A study recently released by the Departments of Labor, Commerce and Education reports that two-thirds of 134 employers surveyed found that new employees lacked basic skills in math, writing, problem solving, and communication.

These statistics indicate that secular humanism not only invaded our public schools with the introduction of progressive education, but also invaded the minds of our children.

The invasion of humanism, and its five cardinal doctrines—man-centered thinking, atheism, evolution, amorality, and the socialist one-worldview—have resulted in our children's disillusionment with America, rebellion toward God and parental authority, a tragic lack of skills, and a loss of self-worth, purpose, and happiness.

As an example of what our schools are teaching, let me share with you an incident that occurred in a public school in Missoula, Montana. Last February the administration of a particular junior high school gave valentines to every student. But these were not ordinary valentines. On the front, they said "love carefully" and, when opened, they revealed a condom. The message: "Love carefully and here's your safe-sex condom." The *underlying* message imparted to these *junior high students* was "Of course you are going to be sexually active so here's your means of loving carefully."

These irresponsible and dangerous messages are also perpetuated in many public schools by the indoctrinating "services" of Planned Parenthood.

When students who come from homes with morals are thrust into a situation that exposes them to *actions* and *values* absolutely contrary to what they are taught at home, the result is a sense of betrayal.

The American public can no longer be deceived by the claim that our public school system is value-neutral. America's children are learning values. They are learning that they are free to read books containing verbally pornographic material, but it is wrong to read their Bibles. They are learning that it is wrong to speak of God, but it is fine to talk freely about and participate in sexual activity. They cannot pray to their Creator, but they can participate in hedonistic activities. It is okay to ridicule Christian thought, but do not make judgments regarding homosexuality or bisexuality or a woman's right to kill her unborn child.

Dr. James Parsons, a Christian psychologist in Florida, states: "Modern sex education is creating such an obsession with sex that it leaves the student little time or interest in either spiritual or academic pursuits."

Is it any wonder that we have the illiteracy rate that we do today? Is it any wonder that our educational system has deteriorated to such a degree?

As we look toward the future, I would like to share with you a familiar quote from *The Humanist* magazine (January-February 1983). It states:

> I am convinced that the battle for humankind's future must be waged and won in the public school classroom . . . by teachers . . . who correctly perceive their role as proselytizers of a new faith: a religion of humanity . . . that recognizes and respects what theologians call the divinity of every human being.
>
> These teachers must embody the same selfless dedication as the most rabid fundamentalist preachers, for they will be ministers of another sort . . . utilizing the classroom instead of the pulpit . . . to convey the humanist values in whatever subject they teach . . . regardless of the educational level— preschool, day care center, or large state university.
>
> The classroom must and will become an arena of conflict between the old and the new—the rotting

corpse of Christianity . . . and the new faith of Humanism. . . . It will undoubtedly be a long, arduous, painful struggle replete with much sorrow and many tears, but humanism will emerge triumphant.

A chilling statement to say the least. Make no mistake, this statement embodies the humanists' vision for the future. If we allow the humanists to maintain control, our public school children will graduate little more than socialist and humanist ideologues, preoccupied with their attitudes, feelings, and sexuality.

But I do not believe this vision will become reality, because of people like you who will not sit idly by and allow it to happen in America.

As we prepare for the year 2020, we will have to get involved in our educational system, in our local school boards. We will have to take the time to sit down with administrators and teachers and be willing to read curricula. And, above all, we must commit ourselves to reestablishing the moral environment conducive to learning.

Praise God there are concerned people like you who are willing to become informed, people willing to accept the challenge of returning to their communities to take action. We must realize that the humanists are waging their battle in our public schools. If America is to survive, Christians must battle on that same ground for a return to the Biblical principles upon which this great country was founded.

In closing, I leave you with this quote from George Washington. He said:

Of all the dispositions and habits which lead to political prosperity, religion and morality are indispensable supports. . . . And let us with caution indulge the supposition that morality can be maintained without religion. . . . Reason and experience both forbid us to expect that national morality can prevail in exclusion of religious principle.

FOCUS POINTS

1. What were the original purposes of American public education?

2. Why was education not embodied in the Constitution?

3. What was the educational mission of the progressives?

4. What has been the result of the invasion of humanism in public education? Cite specific examples.

5. What must Christians do *now* to begin to win the battle against humanism in the schools?

6. What can *you* do?

10

VICTIMIZING OUR CHILDREN

Beverly LaHaye

This speech given in 1988 at CWA's fifth annual convention, focuses on our primary concern, our battle for America's children. They are being victimized by government, by medicine, by education, and by special interest groups. I issued a call to action to those in attendance, and that challenge now goes forth to all the readers of this book.

Concerned Women for America is nine years old. CWA be celebrating our tenth anniversary next year, and our motto from the very beginning has been "protecting the rights of the family through prayer and action"—in that order.

We believe that prayer is important before you act. If we act in our own strength, then we'll move in our own strength. But when we pray and then act, we move in God's strength.

We've experienced many victories for families in the courts and in legislation. CWA strives to follow the example the Word of God sets for us regarding the priority placed upon the family. This organization stands strong for the family, strong for the children.

The psalmist says children are a heritage from the Lord, a gift from the Lord (see Psalm 127:3). In Matthew 19, Jesus says, "Let the little children alone, and do not hinder them from coming to Me; for the kingdom of heaven belongs to such as these" (19:14, NAS). And in Matthew 18:6, He says: "Whoever causes one of these little ones who believe in Me to stumble, it is better for him that a millstone be hung around his neck, and that he be drown in the depth of the sea," (NAS).

During the next thirty minutes that I will be speaking to you tonight:

- thirty youths will attempt suicide;
- 315 youths will decide to quit school;
- 1850 high school seniors will smoke marijuana;
- sixty teenage girls will become pregnant;
- fifteen will give birth to illegitimate babies;
- twenty-four will have abortions.

We are building a society where children no longer feel the security and the value that the Lord has placed on them. The American home has changed from the central haven of comfort, rest, and security to a bed and breakfast.

This year one of the main topics of political issues and discussions has been what kind of child care should the government subsidize and who will care for the babies. We are told that in our economy we cannot live on one income, so mothers must work. When mothers work, we need child care.

No longer is the priority put on the child. The question is: Will government become the mothers and fathers of today's American children? A step in the advance of man's wisdom only creates other problems.

Who are the victims? The children are the victims.

The value of human life has been at the forefront of the battle for several years. During the next three days of our convention, approximately twelve thousand unborn babies will be aborted—that's four thousand a day or 1.5 million a year.

To add to this outrage and the assault on human dignity, we have the increasing use of human fetal tissue for experimentation. This medical holocaust has advanced to the use of tissues and organs not only from fetuses but also from newborn babies as well. I am speaking of human tissue harvested from aborted babies or organs taken from the bodies of brain-impaired newborns (encephalic babies whose brains are not really considered brain dead). The intent: to help patients with Parkinson's disease.

Introducing these medical problems and procedures only opens the door to the cutting of ethical corners in order to reap organs before they deteriorate. Bills introduced in the state legislatures of Ohio and California call for redefining the word *dead* for purposes of organ transplants to accommodate the harvesting of organs. Once this terrible procedure becomes widespread and enters the marketplace, we will see a whole new industry based upon immoral values and the exploitation of women and children.

Dr. Jack Willke, president of the National Right to Life, calls the fetal tissue transplant procedure "fatally flawed" because its source is an innocent unborn baby.

Who are the victims? Children are the victims.

What about education in our public schools? We would think that certainly there the child can learn. Certainly there the child can build for the future and have a feeling of security and self-worth. Certainly?

In science class, our children are taught evolution rather than creation, ruling out the existence of God.

In 1962, prayer was removed from the classrooms largely through the efforts of one atheistic woman.

In social studies children are taught global education which communicates to children that the traditional Judeo-Christian ideals of America are no longer valid as absolutes in a multi-cultural society with a myriad of "equally sound" ideals.

In some health or "family life" classes, a sex quotient test is administered to determine the student's male or female direction. In some programs, students are told that one out of every ten will be a homosexual; and, therefore, they need to learn the lifestyle of a homosexual. "Project 10" is one such program.

But let a student speak for herself. In the book *Grand Illusions: The Legacy of Planned Parenthood*, author George Grant shares an interview with a young girl. I don't like to read this, but I will so you can hear it straight from her:

> She tells the story of second period Tuesday and Thursdays. It was "Health" class. This week, a representative of Planned Parenthood had come to talk about sex, contraception, pregnancy, and abortion.

"At first I couldn't tell where all this was leading," Catherine said. "But then it became really obvious. She [the woman from Planned Parenthood] started asking us personal questions—very personal questions. Like about our feelings, about sex, and even about . . . well about masturbation. It was so disgusting. All the boys were giggling but you could tell that even they were embarrassed."

Then she showed us a film that was extremely explicit. An unashamedly brash couple fondled one another in preparation for intercourse. At an appropriate moment of interest, the camera zoomed in for close-up shots—sweaty body parts rubbing, caressing, kissing, stroking, petting, embracing. At the height of passion, the camera fixed on the woman's hands, trembling as she tore open a condom package, and began to slowly unroll its contents onto her partner.

When the lights came back on, the entire class was visibly shaken. With eyes as wide as saucers, the youngsters sat speechless and amazed.

But their guest was entirely non-plussed.

"She began to tell us that everything we had just seen was totally normal and totally good. She said that the couple obviously had a caring, loving, and responsible relationship—because they took proper precautions against conception and disease."

At that, the teacher passed several packages around the room—one for each of the girls. She instructed the boys to hold up a finger so that the girls could practice contraceptive application.

Already shell-shocked, the students did as they were told.

Afterwards, several of the girls began quietly sobbing; another ran out of the room and threw up; still another fainted. Mercifully, the class ended just a moment later.

Catherine closed her interview by saying, "I have never been more humiliated in all my life. I felt dirty and defiled after seeing the film. But then, when I had to put that thing on Billy's finger, that was just awful. It was horrible. It was like I'd been raped. Raped in my mind. Raped by my school. Raped by Planned Parenthood. I think I was—that we have all been betrayed."

You have just sat through a "health" class that is taking place on some campuses in America. I was shocked by this. This is not the literature that we like to sit down and read. But ladies and gentlemen, our young people in many schools are facing this very thing. We need to be shocked. We need to be awakened to what's happening to our young people. They are the ones who are the victims.

School sex clinics pass out free contraceptives, counsel on abortion, and taxi students to the clinics without parental notification.

In language class, students discuss idiomatic statements relating to death and dying.

In economics, they participate in the lifeboat exercise which requires them to place a value on each person's life and leads them to believe that their worth is determined by their peers.

In English class, students are asked to write their own obituary.

In government, many of our children are taught that there is no difference between America and the Soviet Union, thus thrusting them into an insidious form of ideological warfare.

In ethics, they are taught that the values of honesty and morality are subject to their own interpreta-

tion. God and His Word are irrelevant. Self is supreme.

Each of these exercises or courses of study places
a burden on the child that he or she is spiritually and
emotionally unable to handle. The result: their faith
and their hope are stripped from them, from their
young hearts.

Who are the victims? Our children are the victims.

And we wonder today why so many thousands
of children are attempting suicide. Youth suicides
have increased 253 percent in the last twenty-five
years, or 10.5 percent every year. We are not giving
our children hope for life, a feeling of self-worth, a
reason for living, a purpose.

The subjects could go on and on. Time will not
permit me to touch on them all. But one more of vital
importance is the teaching of our children about
communism.

Secretary of Education William Bennett asked
these questions: Are we teaching our young Americans to understand why the Berlin Wall was created?
Do they know what the dictatorship of the proletariat
means? Can they grasp the significance of a totalitarian state?

In 1986, it was Gary Bauer, then under secretary
of education, who analyzed six major history texts
that were released by major publishers during the
years of 1983 through 1985. He concluded that all six
texts were "hypercritical of the American system,
glossed over the intrinsic character of totalitarian
government, made no critical distinctions between
the two countries, and presented them as equal." Un-
derstandably, our children have no frame of reference to draw upon what will assist them in under-

standing the significance of the Nicaraguan situation
or the invasion of Afghanistan.

A recent survey by Gallup pollsters, in concert
with *National Geographic* magazine, tested teachers and
students on geography and current events and found
that only one-half of those tested knew that the con-
tras and Sandinistas were fighting in Nicaragua. Communism is at our back door and teachers and students
are uninformed, unaware, or disinterested.

CWA has diligently tried to educate our members
on the intrusion of communism in our hemisphere.
In fact, just recently, in traveling to the West Coast. I
met a lady who recognized me and said, "I'm a
member of CWA, I get your newsletter, and I read
every issue from cover to cover." And she related a
story to me concerning her minister's efforts to organize a church group to travel to Nicaragua and assist
the Sandinistas. She said that when she heard her
minister's announcement, she was appalled. She returned home that Sunday, cut out a number of related articles from our newsletter, delivered them to
her minister, and asked that he read them before re-
suming preparations for the trip. He agreed and, as a
result of our articles, the trip has been delayed until
further research is done.

This is a perfect example of the lack of education
on communism. Ladies and gentlemen, this conflict
is taking place just two hours from our borders, and
our children are sure to be the victims if we don't do
something about communism.

Former Secretary of State George Shultz, upon his
return from a recent trip to Central and South America, made this statement (one which I support whole-
heartedly): "Nicaragua is a threat to the United

States, a cancer that the United States must cut out before it spreads." And if it is not, our children will be the victims.

Finally, let me touch briefly on the ACLU, or the American Civil Liberties Union, an organization that is helping to destroy our children. We hear much about the ACLU today because one of our presidential candidates in 1988 admitted that he is a card-carrying member. The ACLU has a secret membership of 250,000. It has a board of directors that constitutes the official voice of the union and has put out a policy guide as its basis for action. Let me give you just a few of the guidelines:

- Policy Number 4 urges repeal of all laws against pornography. While the ACLU opposes the taking of obscene pictures of children, it defends those who sell, distribute, and profit from child pornography, making the ACLU the leading ideological protector of the giant smut industry of the United States.

- Policy Number 18 calls for ending the private rating systems of movies because the G, PG, PG-13, R, and X ratings (designed to protect children from dirty and violent films) "have a chilling effect on the freedom of expression."

- Policy Number 81 calls for a permanent ban on displays of the nativity scene and the menorah on public property.

- Policy Number 84 calls for the removal of "under God" from the Pledge of Allegiance.

- Policy Number 92 calls for an end to tax exemptions for all churches and synagogues.

- Policy Number 210 calls for the legalization of all narcotics, including crack cocaine and angel dust, contending that the "introduction of substances into one's own body" is a civil liberty.

- Policy Number 242 urges that "all criminals except those guilty of such crimes as murder and treason . . . be given a suspended sentence . . . and be sent back to the community."

- Policy No. 264 (supported by ACLU lawsuits) declares that gays have a constitutional right to marry, become foster parents and engage in street solicitation.

Ladies and gentlemen, we are in a battle, a battle for our children. And many Americans, many Christian Americans, are not even aware that a battle rages around us. Scripture says: "For our struggle is not against flesh and blood, but against the rulers, against the powers, against the world forces of this darkness, against the spiritual forces of wickedness in the heavenly places" (Ephesians 6:12, NAS). That is the battle that we have before us.

What is our hope?

Permit me to refer to a story in the Old Testament, the story of Rachel. Jeremiah 31:15 tells about Rachel who is so burdened for her children that she weeps for them because they are no more. Our circumstances may be different but the principles and the promise here are the same. The Lord says to Rachel, "Refrain your voice from weeping, and your eyes from tears; for your work shall be rewarded. . . . There is hope for your future . . . your children shall return to their own territory" (Jeremiah 31:16–17, NAS).

As I study this Scripture, I see it as hope for CWA. *We should be weeping for our children,* and not just those within our four walls, but America's children. We are developing, building, and preparing the leaders of tomorrow under constant threat. Yet the Scripture says your efforts—your work—will be rewarded.

That is our hope. We cannot sit back and allow ourselves to fall prey to apathy or indifference. We still must work.

Are you part of a prayer chapter? If you are only involved in the battle and not praying, then you are a prime target for discouragement. You need to be involved in a prayer chapter. If there is not one close by, build one. Go to your area leader and tell her you want to help.

This is a battle, and the Lord says your efforts will be rewarded. You need to be praying for your children and America's children.

I hear all sorts of excuses as I travel. I think I've heard them all. Each time I hear one, I am reminded of a story from the Korean War.

A captain had his headquarters behind the front lines. One day, as the captain was working in his tent, a corporal came rushing in. He looked dirty and battle weary as he breathlessly reported, "Sir, I need your help. I have a problem."

The captain responded, "What is your problem?"

The corporal replied, "Sir, my men are pinned down with sniper fire; they've been abandoned. They have had no food for three days, and we need to send a rescue party. If not, we'll lose the territory and the men."

The captain said, "I hear you."

At that same moment, another corporal rushed into the tent and said, "Sir, I have a problem."

And the captain asked, "What is your problem?"

The corporal said, "Sir, my tent leaks."

The message I want you to glean from this story is that I can tell where you are in the battle by what your complaints are, by what your excuses are.

We can all think of excuses. We can all think of reasons why. But there is still a battle raging. The Lord says that it will be your work, your efforts that He will reward. I challenge you while there is still time to get into the battle lest your children become the victims.

One day, one glorious day, the battle will be over. But until then we must work to protect America's children. And our hope is that promise that one day the Lord will say, "It is finished. The battle is over."

FOCUS POINTS

1. How does our government threaten our children?

2. How are children victimized by the medical profession?

3. In this speech, ten examples from school curricula are given as illustrations of how education can victimize children. Cite at least five of them.

4. How is it possible for churches to victimize children?

5. Pretend you are on a television debate program with a member of the ACLU. Marshal
   your arguments why you oppose the stance
   of the ACLU to policy numbers 4, 18, 81,
   84, 92, 210, 242, and 264.

6. Consider what you can personally do to
   fight the battle to protect America's children. Do you really have any valid excuses
   for inaction?

11

THE CASE FOR CHRISTIAN EDUCATION

Albert Veldhuyzen

To combat unsavory influences in public schools, many parents are opting for private Christian schools or, increasingly, home schooling. Presented here are reasons for this trend.

The academic and moral quality of American education has consistently deteriorated during the last few decades. It has become a recognized fact that most American students are academically inferior to their counterparts in Japan and many European countries. Because of the wholesale purging of morality from our secular institutions, students have also lost a sense of right and wrong. The behavioral consequences have been noted by even the staunchest defenders of state education.

As reported in the *Washington Post* of June 2, 1987, the Forum of Educational Organization Leaders, an organization encompassing public school boards, teachers, and administrators, concluded that a "radical change" has occurred in the nature of American students. Among other facts, the Forum said that the birthrate of U.S. teenagers is twice that of any other Western nation, and delinquency among ten- to seventeen-year-olds has increased 130 percent since 1960. Another disturbing fact is that our drug use is the highest of any industrialized nation.

One of the reasons for these alarming statistics is that the old morality, solidly rooted in our Christian foundations, is no longer taught to the children. A child is often told to develop his own personal values without parental and religious influences. Abortion, suicide, euthanasia, and homosexuality are presented as viable and positive alternative personal choices.

For example, by sheltering "health" clinics that provide contraceptives free of charge in many of our schools and outside the reach of parental control, the state has implicitly encouraged teenage promiscuity.

In the case of sex education, Phyllis Schlafly discusses the merits of a prototypical sex education program in her book *Child Abuse in the Classroom.* She says that "being a public school course, sexual education programs do not tell pupils that premarital sex is wrong; the teacher would be forbidden to do that. Instead, the pupil is instructed to 'identify and evaluate the choices involved in sexual expression.' "

Another example of the results of declining morals is the increase of violence and vandalism in the schools. In 1965 there were no security guards in

Chicago schools. Today there are more than seven hundred.

The question to be asked is whether parents in good faith can send their children to be taught humanistic propaganda in such unhealthy surroundings. Thousands of parents have come to the conclusion that they cannot and have enrolled their children in Christian schools. Some parents have decided to teach their children at home. The recently open and blatant bias against the religious values held by many, and demonstrated anew by the Supreme Court decision to censor creationism in the state schools, will cause more parents to take their children out of state schools.

The Scriptures tell parents to "train up a child in the way he should go, even when he is old he will not depart from it" (Proverbs 22:6). Parents, not the state, have the God-given responsibility for the education of their children.

Home-school advocates point to studies that show how early institutionalization can have harmful effects on children. Dale Farran of the University of North Carolina reports that day-care children display negative aggressive acts fifteen times as often as home-care youngsters. Urie Bronfenbrenner of Cornell University says that children who spend more time with their peers than with their parents become peer dependent. Sending children to state schools also exposes their impressionable young minds to unchristian peer values which can easily result in low self-worth, low optimism, and low respect for parents.

But even worse than negative peer values are the secular humanist ethics taught by many public school teachers. John Dunphy, writing in *The Humanist* magazine of January/February 1983, frankly laid out the strategy and goals of the secular humanists. He states:

> The battle for humankind's future must be waged and won in the public school classroom by teachers who correctly perceive their role as the proselytizers of a new faith. . . . These teachers must embody the same selfless dedication as the most rabid fundamentalist preachers, for they will be ministers of another sort, utilizing a classroom instead of a pulpit to convey humanist values in whatever subject they teach, regardless of the educational level.

This "religion of humanity" denies absolute Biblical values and upholds moral relativism. But just as secular humanism encompasses all areas of life and every academic discipline, so does the gospel. The Bible presents a comprehensive world and life view which individuals and societies are commanded to obey. Christian children ought to be made aware of other moral viewpoints and lifestyles. But they need to be taught to reject evil and shown the path to follow. In every subject, the child should be confronted with the Biblical evidence and shown the comprehensive nature of Christ's demands on his life and thought processes. The moral "neutrality" in the state schools precludes such necessary education.

Deuteronomy 6:6-7 states that "these words which I command you today shall be in your heart. You shall teach them diligently to your children, and shall talk of them when you sit in your house, when you walk by the way, when you lie down, and when you rise up."

In the environment of many schools, it is hard to expect youngsters to "witness" and effectively battle the myriad of humanistic concepts being taught.

Christian parents who have opted out of the government school system have chosen home schooling rather than private Christian schools for many reasons. One reason to choose home schooling is that it is more affordable than private schools. Home-education materials cost only a few hundred dollars, whereas private schools cost thousands of dollars.

Professional educators have spread the myth that home-schooled children are being deprived of a quality education. But statistics show the opposite is true. Academically, Christian-school and home-school students perform much better than those attending state schools. According to *USA Today* of May 15, 1985, "Alaska and Arizona, which test home-schooled children, report that they perform above average on nationally standardized tests. These kids appear to make up for socialization missed in school through scouting and other activities." Unlike public education, the term "functional illiterate" is unheard of among home schoolers.

Many of the world's great minds were shaped in a home classroom: Winston Churchill, Konrad Adenauer, Douglas MacArthur, George Patton, Agatha Christie, Abraham Lincoln, and Woodrow Wilson. Supreme Court Justice Sandra Day O'Connor was home schooled until age nine.

Home schooling also allows parents greater control and more options in the choice of curricula. Other advantages of home schooling include low student-to-teacher ratio, scheduling flexibility, and greater family unity.

The Reverend Paul D. Lindstrom heads the largest home-school system in the United States with over twenty-thousand enrolled students. He says, "The home-schooled students also tend to do very well in college because they know how to study. They have that inner self-discipline because they have been involved with self-directed study for many years."

Graduates of the Reverend Lindstrom's Christian Liberty Academy Satellite Schools* can follow the same courseload and receive the same degrees as those completing his kindergarten through twelfth grade traditional day-school program in Arlington Heights, Illinois.

Various states handle their laws differently in the area of home schooling, regulating them in varying degrees. But the concept itself has been repeatedly upheld as a basic constitutional right.† In *Pierce v. Society of Sisters*, the U.S. Supreme Court declared:

> The fundamental theory of liberty upon which all governments in this Union repose excludes any general power of the State to standardize its children by forcing them to accept instruction from public teachers only. The child is not the mere creature of the state; those who nurture him and direct his destiny have the right, coupled with the high duty, to recognize and prepare him for additional obligations.

---

* For more information, contact: Christian Liberty Academy, 502 W. Euclid Avenue, Arlington Heights, IL 60004, (312) 259-8736.

† For a summary of education edicts in each of the fifty states, contact: Home School Legal Defense Association, Paeonian Springs, VA 22129, (703) 882-3838.

Both private Christian schools and home education are booming because Christians are becoming more conscious of the Biblical mandate to impart a holistic God-centered education to their children. Parents are seeing the increasingly prevalent corruption, violence, poor academic standards, and anti-Christian education in the state schools.

If we are serious about reclaiming our culture for Christ, we need to develop an infrastructure of Biblically based law, science, art, and politics. We need a cadre of men and women willing to fashion their lives and their society according to such principles. Christian education is intrinsic in God's will for the lives of his people and their children.

FOCUS POINTS

1. For what specific reasons have some parents chosen not to send their children to public schools?

2. Compare a home-based education with an institutional one as to (a) cost, (b) quality of education, (c) curriculum content, (d) social, emotional, and moral growth, (e) standardized test results, (f) college performance.

3. Write for further information regarding curriculum for home schooling and the laws relative to home schooling in your area.

4. Assess the present education of your child, both the pluses and the minuses. What do you find?

12

WHAT REALLY HAPPENS TO CHILDREN WHEN THEY GO TO PUBLIC SCHOOLS

Dr. Tim LaHaye

It must be said. The public has a right to know. With a national drive now focused on improvement of America's educational system, citizens need to read the facts to see where we are now, what we are really dealing with. More and more concerned parents are opting out of public education, but responsible people are still concerned about all the children who remain in it.

L ast fall, four million innocent five-year-olds entered kindergarten across America. Their little eyes betrayed their fear or excitement, whatever may have been the case; their parents, sometimes teary-eyed, were eager with expectation that these children receive an education to prepare them both to be productive citizens and to meet the challenges of life.

Let's look at what can really be expected from today's education, according to current statistics:

- One million girls, almost 50 percent of teenage girls, will become pregnant out of wedlock, before graduation day.

- One million four hundred thousand boys, or 70 percent, will become sexually active before they leave high school.

- 85 percent of the children entering school will be taught the "look-say" reading method instead of the phonetic approach. That is why one million two hundred thousand children—29 percent—will be functionally illiterate by graduation.

- Most of these children will not learn to write well, and some will not learn to write at all.

- Six hundred thousand of these children—15 percent—will become so disillusioned with school that they will drop out.

- More than one million two hundred thousand—one third of all school children—will be so poorly educated that they will needlessly function below their intelligence potential for all their adult lives.

- Most will do poorly at math, and many will fail to learn to add, multiply, or divide.

- All of these children will be taught the theory of evolution, and many will be told it is a fact of science. Few will learn that there is more scientific evidence to support creationism—the belief that man was really created by God. Consequently, these children will be led to believe they are animals; and, therefore, they should be free to do anything their animal appetites desire.

- Many of these children will be exposed to as many as 180 hours of very explicit sex education courses, held in mixed classes without benefit of moral values—which has helped create the national obsession for sex in teenagers' lives at a time when they really need an obsession for learning.

- Most of these children will be exposed to at least one or more teachers who are best described as "change agents." That is, they will be schooled in the art of "Values Clarification," which is a scientific assault on the moral values the child was taught at home and in his church. Usually this is not a specific course but is infiltrated into several existing classes such as literature, history, health, or others.

- Only about 50 percent will learn enough geography to be able to identify the location of Chicago, Miami, Fort Worth, and Portland. Even fewer will be able to locate places like Germany, Spain, or China.

- Many will take a course in "death and dying," which not only gives atheist teachers an ideal opportunity to attack any Biblical or Christian doctrines they choose, but also teaches students the four most successful methods of committing suicide.

- The majority of these four million children will, during their thirteen years of public school, be exposed to violence, crime, lack of discipline, and, of course, drugs of every kind—at a time when

peer pressure is greater than at any other time in
history.

- And of course, the child will be taught "one-
  world globalism" instead of patriotic American-
  ism. Communism and socialism will be presented in the best possible light, and capitalism
  will be taught as a greed-motivated economic system that is largely responsible for the poverty of
  the Third World countries.

- Environmentalism and a nuclear attack by the
  super powers will be presented as the singularly
  most dangerous thing in the world, and that any
  compromise is better than precipitating a nuclear
  explosion—even the loss of freedom.

- Soviet Russia and other communist countries will
  be presented as respectable and a moral equivalent of the United States. They will not be blamed
  for world unrest; their systematic murder of millions of their own people enroute to subjugating
  their citizens will be glossed over or not told at
  all; nor will their consistent pattern of violating
  signed treaties be mentioned.

- These children will not be taught the truth about
  the religious heritage of this nation, nor will they
  be permitted to see religious symbols on the
  walls of the schools—even the Ten Command-
  ments have been removed by decision of the
  courts.

- Many will be exposed to the teachings of new
  age, yoga, transcendental meditation, witchcraft
  demonstrations, and Eastern religions—while
  any mention of God, Jesus Christ, Christianity,
  the Bible, and prayer is forbidden.

• Not a few of these children during their thirteen
  years of education will be exposed to homosexu-
  als or lesbians as teachers or other role models.
  Many will be taught that such sexual practices
  are normal and healthy. Some curricula even suggest that as many as 10 percent of the students
  are probably prone to be homosexual and should
  be open to consider the alternate sexual lifestyle.

This inferior education will cost taxpayers over
357 billion dollars annually—between forty-five hundred to six thousand dollars per student.

But that is not the greatest price parents pay for
free public education. The greatest price is the dam-
age done to the mind of their child. His education is
inferior; his values twisted. He may well become hostile to his parents, God, and society because liberalism—the official secular humanist philosophy of our
public schools—produces rebels. And he will be ill-
prepared for life and poorly equipped to make the
important choices of college, marriage, or a vocation.

A "mind is a terrible thing to waste" is not just a
good slogan; it should be the attitude of every parent. As a minister, author, and educator who has
watched public education for over forty years, I have
come to the reluctant conclusion that the best way to
waste or possibly pervert your child's mind is to subject it to the public school for thirteen years. For
Christian parents, it can be a disaster. I have further
come to the conclusion that the public school, as it is
constituted today in many communities, is unfit for
the minds of children from Christian homes. It is
only fit for mature Christian adults who, as qualified
teachers and administrators, remain in the system to
perform the work of a missionary to serve their Lord

and their country in providing as much positive influence as possible, and to do their best to offset the above-mentioned travesties in the name of education.

Christian parents have an alternative—Christian schools or home schools—where their children can receive a Bible-based education that usually produces better results than most public schools. The environment is supportive and the child's role models will be Christian; their peer pressure will be similar to that which they have at church; and they will be challenged to invest their lives vocationally, mentally, and physically for Jesus Christ.

Yes, it may cost money for tuition or curriculum materials, but it may well be the best investment you will ever make for your child—protecting and directing the mind, soul, and body of your children in "the way he should go." If the Lord tarries, it will stand him in good stead the rest of his life.

FOCUS POINTS

1. Why do you think our public education system is in such a sorry plight?

2. How can America prevent "wasting" the minds of its youth?

3. What is the situation in your local school system?

4. What can you do?

13

SEX EDUCATION IN AMERICA: WHOSE VALUES ARE TAUGHT?

Kimberly Parker

A course in "health" would seem innocuous for young people to study in school. But sometimes it covers very explicit sexual content. Many parents welcome having concepts of "family living" and "sex education" offered for study but are appalled to find they espouse practices and values totally at odds with their moral orientation. To be forewarned is to be forearmed. Read here some examples of what has occurred so you can protect your children from deplorable brainwashing.

For nearly two decades, organizations like the Sex Information and Education Council of the United States (SIECUS) and Planned Parenthood have cited *ad nauseam* opinion polls indicating overwhelming parental approval of comprehensive sex education. Impressive yet questionable statistics are employed to convince the American public that the vast majority of parents recognize the necessity of comprehensive sex education and welcome the opportunity for their children to receive "expert" instruction.

However, the issue so skillfully evaded by these organizations is whether parents and educators agree on the *content* of this comprehensive sex education. Is there a difference in what parents expect and what their children are forced to endure? The intense disputes occurring nationwide over the content of "human sexuality" or "family life" courses suggest that differences do indeed exist.

Parents who sign permission slips for these courses, expecting their children to receive a scientific explanation of human reproduction and learn the dangers of premarital sexual activity, have been deceived. The new sex education philosophy strays far from human anatomy and biological reproduction. Prominent sex educator Mary Lee Tatum of Falls Church, Virginia, says, "When I say anatomy and physiology, I mean sexual response—erections, orgasms, all those good things. But that's not what *they* [parents] mean at all."

Sex education courses in many areas of the country are nothing short of how-to seminars where anything goes. Preschoolers learn explicit genital terminology and preadolescents learn about homosexuality, masturbation, erections, and nocturnal emissions. Teens review the same material augmented by a battery of exercises that assault their values and emotions and desensitize them to perverse practices.

Why the change in sex education? Because the advocates of this comprehensive sex education are after the hearts and minds of America's children.

In an address titled "The Case for Moral Education in the Schools," Sol Gordon, one of the leading sex educators in the country, frankly admits, "I sometimes wonder if we sex educators don't deserve some of the bad media coverage we've seen lately. Why is it so difficult for us to say that we are unequivocally in support of a moral sexuality education? A sex education without values is valueless. Of course we endorse a value-laden, moral sex education—but whose values? Ours."

Toward this end, these sex peddlers have pushed for changes in instruction and curriculum. Materials and presentations vary in their explicit detail, but they do not differ in their undermining of moral values.

There are two standard themes that persist throughout most texts and discussions. The first is the "enlightened" view that all sexual practices are equivalent in their morality and normality. Purveyors of this idea say no sexual practice is deviant. Propaganda from the homosexual movement is standard fare, and teachers are encouraged by their education instructors to "clean up their homosexist language."

In Virginia, a video, *On Being Gay*, has been circulated and used by some schools. In this film, Brian McNaught, the homosexual host, requests that viewers participate in an exercise imagining themselves as breeders (heterosexuals) in an all-gay world. This exercise attempts to equate homosexuality with heterosexuality and create sympathy for the "victimized" homosexual who is simply acting on his or her "natural feelings."

The second theme is that people are sexual from birth and should not be discouraged from expressing their sexuality at any age. Parental authority is undermined and adherence to Biblical absolutes is ridiculed. Some teenagers have received failing grades for particular exercises when they based their actions and solutions upon Biblical values.

Texts of this new philosophy are designed to destroy family values, desensitize teenagers to "once-forbidden" activities, and demystify sex by explaining how certain activities are performed. Wardell Pomeroy's *Boys and Sex*, hawked by Planned Parenthood as an appropriate book for teens, states, "Premarital intercourse does have its definite values as a training ground for marriage or some other committed relationship. . . . It's a big help in finding out whether they are really congenial or not; to make an everyday comparison again, it's like taking a car out for a test run before you buy it."

Pomeroy's *Girls and Sex* asserts, "For those who plan on marriage eventually, early intercourse can also be a training ground. . . . There are many girls who regret after marriage that they didn't have premarital intercourse, because they've come to realize what a long, slow learning process it can often be after marriage."

In *Changing Bodies, Changing Lives*, another Planned Parenthood favorite, Ruth Bell uses quotes from sex-driven teenagers to present every form of sexual activity and the feelings that accompany each. The author explains masturbation, oral sex, anal sex, how to apply a condom, and offers hints on how to enjoy fornication without becoming pregnant. Hardly anything is left to the imagination and no perversion is excluded.

Instructors are encouraged to employ techniques such as "values clarification," "role playing," and "sensitivity training" to erode sexual inhibitions and undermine family values. Some teachers take their children on guided fantasies designed to sexually excite and play board games where teenagers receive sexual gratification points for choosing sexual intercourse.

Parents frequently will receive notices regarding lectures on seemingly benign topics, only to realize later that their children were subjected to a form of emotional abuse.

In Arlington County, Virginia, the parents of sixth and seventh graders at one public school were informed that a speaker had been invited to address their children on human growth and development. What ensued, however, was an obscene discussion that undermined parental authority and encouraged promiscuity. The speaker, a pediatrician from Children's Hospital, did not exercise judgment in the appropriateness of the material, nor was she hindered by the obvious embarrassment of the students. The subjects covered included breast development in boys and girls, enlargement of the testicles, nocturnal emissions, vaginal secretions, erections, graphic descriptions of anal sex, and bestiality.

In discussing the appropriate time for sex, Dr. Woodward said, "Parents will say after you are married and you have a college education and have your own home, but your parents didn't wait that long. So even though they want you to wait, you have to choose the time that is right for you."

When asked a question regarding bestiality, she responded, "People who live on farms discuss other people having sex with animals, sheep. . . . It's been said that when Christopher Columbus came to America, he was so hard up to have sex that he had sex with Indians and sheep."

This new philosophy is not isolated to certain areas of the country. Studies indicate that 75 percent of this nation's school districts are teaching this type of sex education, resulting in the victimization of millions of teenagers each year. This victimization has manifested itself over the last two decades in the 90 percent increase in teen pregnancies, the 230 percent rise in teen abortions, and the 140 percent increase in the reported cases of venereal disease.

Whether the curriculum is labeled "family life," "human sexuality," or simply "health," the instructional materials should be extensively reviewed by parents and the teachers strictly supervised. For that matter, the onslaught of moral relativism should be monitored in all curricula.

Parents must re-embrace their obligation to be the primary educators of their children. Those who refuse this responsibility should call the nearest Planned Parenthood office and offer to be a statistic in their next poll.

FOCUS POINTS

1. Call your local board of education and set up appointments with the curriculum coordinators at elementary, middle, and high school levels. Find out which grade levels

and in which courses sex education and family life material are covered.

2. Ask to borrow copies of syllabi or courses of study to read.

3. Call the principal of your child's school and set up an appointment with the teacher(s) of the course(s) containing sex education.

4. Before the meeting consider these questions (and others that may occur to you): What specific topics should be covered in this course? What questions do children of this age have? In what depth should they be answered? What kinds of audio-visual material are appropriate? What kinds of activities would best enhance instruction? What organization and/or guest experts can add to the class? How can acceptable moral values be conveyed?

5. In a friendly, nonthreatening interview with the teacher, try to determine his/her value position, teaching strategies, and educational goals. Ask to see specific lesson plans. Voice your concerns. Make suggestions. Offer support and help.

6. When your child takes the course, discuss objectively each night what transpired in class that day. Encourage a free exchange of ideas and viewpoints. Monitor homework assignments.

7. If you have any apprehensions, discuss them frankly with the teacher. If real prob-

lems develop, document your concerns, enlist support from the parent-teacher organization (surely you belong to it!), and work
with school officials to modify the course,
for the benefit not only of your child but of
all the others in the school.

14

SCHOOL-BASED CLINICS FALSELY CLAIM TO BE THE ANSWER TO TEEN PREGNANCY

The astounding rise in teenage pregnancies and venereal diseases concerns all thinking people. However, misguided efforts by liberals to address the problems through school-based clinics have backfired. Here the facts are presented, with some sinister questions raised.

P lanned Parenthood's influence becomes more conspicuous in our public schools every year. Sex education was its "foot in the door" two decades ago, but it soon realized that classroom assaults were not enough to totally reform the values and beliefs of our nation's youngsters. Now this degenerate organization and its allies are crusading in every school district in the nation.

Parents who faithfully visit their children's schools to converse with teachers and review textbooks had better stop by the administrative offices on the way out and inquire about the possible existence of a *family planning clinic* on school premises. According to the Center for Population Options (CPO), a Planned Parenthood ally, there are close to two hundred school-based clinics currently operating. They are located in thirty-two states and ninety communities. The total represents a five-fold increase since 1983 and the figure continues to grow.

CPO literature states that a school-based clinic is a primary health care center, located on the grounds of middle, junior, and senior high schools, which provides a variety of health and social services to young people as a part of the school day. These services include athletic physicals, general health assessments, laboratory and diagnostic screening (e.g., sickle cell anemia and sexually transmitted disease screening), immunization, family planning counseling and services, drug and alcohol abuse, etc.

Clinic employees and advocates would prefer to concentrate public scrutiny on the services that do not engender as much controversy as family planning. However, behind closed doors, the focus is on reproductive [dis]services. In fact, George Grant, author of *Grand Illusions: The Legacy of Planned Parenthood*, uncovered a 1985 CPO report which contained an article advising that "when a student comes to the clinic ostensibly for other reasons, the clinic can take that opportunity to see if the student wants to discuss sexual behavior and birth control."

A tour of a clinic at a middle school in Baltimore, Maryland, revealed a preoccupation with pushing birth control on youth. Posters advocating the use of contraceptives were plastered throughout the clinic.

One poster read, "Active sportswear for the active man" and pictured a condom. Another advised, "Use condoms. There's living proof they stop AIDS." Not one explicitly mentioned abstinence as the only 100 percent effective approach to preventing pregnancy.

A cursory review of literature available at the Baltimore clinic indicates a similar negligence with respect to discussions of the failure rate of contraceptives. In fact, one CPO brochure available for distribution at clinics advises teens that "latex condoms protect you best from disease—all *will protect* you from pregnancy" (emphasis added).

Displayed on a clinic table was the infamous *The New Our Bodies, Ourselves* book with sections on "defining orgasm" and "learning to masturbate." The book *Changing Bodies, Changing Lives* was also available. A hasty review of this text revealed one section on "exploring sex with someone of the same sex."

Recent survey data distributed at CPO's Sixth Annual School-Based Clinic Conference indicates that 85 percent of the clinics provide counseling on birth control methods, 72 percent offer referrals for birth control methods and exams, 43 percent prescribe contraceptives, and 12 percent dispense contraceptives on site. In addition, 83 percent offer sex education in class, 88 percent offer pregnancy tests, and 83 percent offer pregnancy counseling. Keep in mind that the latter two services certainly provide the forum for abortion counseling and referral.

Operating costs for clinics range from $100,000 to $313,000 per year. The average cost is approximately $125,000. Roughly one-third of the expenses are covered by contributions from private foundations; the other two-thirds comes out of taxpayers' pockets.

According to the CPO survey results, most clinics require parental permission for student participation; some do not. Typically, when parents sign the consent form, their children can receive any of the services. Few clinics allow parents to opt their youngster out of the family planning programs and maintain the remainder of the services. In the clinics that do offer an opt-out provision, parents should make sure that state does not permit students to receive family planning services and treatment for sexually transmitted diseases without parental consent.

Many states currently possess laws that would allow confidential administration of family planning services. Parents should also be aware that notification and consent laws still on the books often go unenforced.

Much to the chagrin of clinic advocates, the recent survey data reveals that the clinics are not having an impact on teen pregnancy. Predictably, clinic proponents attribute failure in this regard to the lack of "comprehensive" services. They claim that the interventions are simply not extensive enough to be successful. Therefore, the failure is used to justify more aggressive outreach programs, sex education in the classroom, and other programs.

Truthfully, these programs fail because they operate on a flawed premise. Clinic advocates believe that every teen has a right to sexual freedom. Therefore, clinics do not target teen illicit sex. They assert that responsible behavior is nothing more than sex with contraceptives.

One must wonder about the motives of those who would continue to advocate "safe sex" when there is overwhelming evidence that contraceptive programs do not reduce teen pregnancy. Dr. Dinah Richard, author of *Teen Pregnancy and Sex Education in the Schools*, cites statistics to show that between 1971 and 1981, federal funding of family planning programs increased 306 percent with a corresponding increase of 48.3 percent in teen pregnancies and a 133 percent rise in abortions for women aged fifteen to nineteen.

Likewise, Dr. Jacqueline Kasun of Humboldt State University found that states with higher-per-capita expenditures on birth control also have higher-than-average teen pregnancy rates.

The explanation for these findings is quite simple. The availability of contraceptives increases teen promiscuity. Two developers of oral contraceptives have admitted this truth. Couple this increase in teen promiscuity with the 10 percent teen contraceptive failure rate (5.8 percent for oral contraceptives), and these programs can do nothing but increase teen pregnancy and, consequently, abortion.

Furthermore, liberal thinkers who refuse to discourage teen promiscuity must acknowledge rises in teen herpes, gonorrhea, syphilis, and AIDS. Substantial evidence also exists linking cervical cancer with early coitus. An article in *Clinics in Obstetrics and Gynecology* states, "There is now convincing evidence that of all the coital factors, age at first intercourse is the most significant and that coitus during early adolescence especially predisposes women to cervical cancer."

Although Planned Parenthood and its allies would deny that they are out to change our children's values and morals, the obvious flaws in this approach does lead on to question their objectives. Could they be more interested in rendering our children dependent on their contraceptive and abortion services than they are in reducing teen pregnancy?

The current climate in our public schools raises the issue of who is actually responsible for the rearing of children. Does Planned Parenthood have the right to tamper with our children's values? Does a nurse practitioner have the right to give children birth control or counsel on abortion without parental consent? It is time that parents let their visibility in the school setting answer these questions for those educators who act as if the "benevolent" state owns America's youngsters.

FOCUS POINTS

1. Does your school system operate family planning clinics on school premises?

2. If so, what services are performed? Tour a clinic, noting posters and reading matter. Interview personnel to find out procedures.

3. What are the laws in your state that might allow confidential administration of family planning services? Are notification and consent laws enforced?

4. Research the figures in your area as to teen pregnancies and per capita expenditures on birth control.

5. Go to Planned Parenthood and get their literature. See what they espouse.

6. If your search warrants it, plan how you and like-minded parents can combat this menace.

15

AIDS EDUCATION WITH A CLEAR MESSAGE OF PREVENTION

Peggy Markell of Ogdensburg, New York, was one of the speakers at a conference on AIDS sponsored by the Alliance for a Sound AIDS Policy. The mother of four and a registered nurse, she gave permission to summarize her talk which explained the major thrust of her work as an educator of youth about AIDS.

D isbelief and complacency are the reactions most often expressed by the young people Peggy Markell speaks with about the deadly disease AIDS. Markell believes that in order to preserve a future generation of young people, "we need to send the optimal message about abstinence."

Markell describes how AIDS has come in two waves in America: first to the homosexual community and secondly to IV drug abusers and minorities.

"The third wave may be heading for our teenagers. But there's time to stop it from occurring," she asserts.

Statistics prove that young people are sexually active and at risk: each day in the United States approximately eleven thousand teens contract a sexually transmitted disease; 25 percent of the reported cases of gonorrhea and syphilis were ten- to nineteen-year-olds; among teen girls, cases of gonorrhea have increased 400 percent. Eighty-eight percent of current AIDS cases are twenty- to forty-nine-year-olds.

Messages like "safe sex" have been ambiguous and unclear, she states. "The emphasis should be changed to avoiding or eliminating the risk of HIV infection, not just reducing the risk. Just reducing the risk of HIV is a 'wimpy' response to a killer disease. Our youth are too precious to lose to what is basically a voluntary epidemic."

Messages about condom use have also been unclear and, therefore, unheeded. "We must realize that condoms are not our first line of defense in HIV prevention. They [condoms] are a *last* resort for individuals who are so deeply entrenched in risk behaviors that they will not change." But most kids are at the experimental stage in sex, Markell says.

The present push of condoms onto teens makes a very unfair assumption that our young people are incapable of self-control, Markell says. "It makes it appear that we've given up on them already."

Contrary to popular opinion, teens' engaging in sex is *not* normal and no amount of statistics will ever make it so, she says. "We need to look for the underlying reason why kids are having sex: low self-esteem, family problems, and lack of skills." Teens lack spiritual and emotional maturity for sexual activity. "Our twenty-year experiment in sex education hasn't worked."

Markell believes that using the word abstinence sends a negative message to teens. Abstinence education does not address the root problem that teens do not attach a high degree of personal risk with HIV, sexually transmitted diseases, or pregnancy. The very word *abstinence* brings to mind the denial of something. Abstinence focuses on one aspect of behavior rather than the whole person.

Buried among the many failed educational attempts is the clear answer: chastity education, says Markell. "It's a great deal more than saying no to premarital sex." Chastity education is learning how to become a loving person who is emotionally mature. "It's about viewing sexuality and fertility as a wonderful gift to be cherished and the proper roles they should play in our lives. Chastity is about respecting and protecting our dignity as human beings who give love and give life," she asserts.

Another difference between abstinence and chastity education is that with abstinence, behavior is changed out of *fear;* with chastity comes a positive attitude toward self and others that results in self-initiated lifestyle changes out of respect and love.

"Most important of all, chastity education has as its foundation the secret ingredient for touching kids' hearts: the development of healthy relationships based on respect, commitment, caring, understanding, trust, and communication." Markell has found that teens identify with relationships because they all feel vulnerable in relationships. "Because of the upheaval in American family life, kids are seeking relationships that are real, where they won't be used, and where they will be accepted for who they are," she says.

The sad commentary, says Markell, is that America has a generation of young people who have never known intimacy. "They are searching and buying into the media's version of intimacy: sex. In America, people in junior and senior high school find it easier to take off their clothes and share their bodies than to take off their masks and share their hopes and fears for fear of rejection."

Chastity reaches the whole person and helps him and her develop skills in communication, patience, understanding, caring, humor, and emotional maturity—all traits needed in chaste dating and marriage, says Markell. "Chastity also capitalizes on unique qualities of youth: creativity, idealism, and the desire to be 'counter cultural.' "

"I don't believe we should be embarrassed about using the word *chastity*. Many times social change begins first with a verbal change," says Markell.

Kids who have been sexually active need an extra special message of encouragement and hope, says Markell. She describes "secondary virginity" as something that happens "when you make the decision to stop sexual involvement from this day forward until marriage." This is important because most teens feel that once they've lost their virginity, what does it matter?

"I give these kids the message of hope that even though they can never regain a virgin body, they can regain a virgin heart. I tell kids that though both are very important, the most important is a virgin heart."

Parents, educators, and concerned citizens must know that "the danger to our young people is real" and we "must take action while there is still time. Let's challenge our young people to chastity and second virginity so they will be survivors of the AIDS holocaust."

FOCUS POINTS

1. Why may the "third wave" of AIDS to hit the United States be heading for our teenagers?

2. Why are standard warnings and traditional approaches ineffective in reaching teenagers?

3. What is the difference between abstinence and chastity?

4. Why is a plea for chastity more powerful than a plea for abstinence?

5. How can committal to "secondary virginity" bestow hope?

6. If the "danger to our young people is real," and "we must take action while there is still time," what action can *you* take?

16

JOHNNY CAN'T READ: WHICH WAY DO WE GO?

Janet and Craig Parshall

Emphasis on the emotional needs of children betrays the fundamental mission of education: to arm our children with the tools through which they can process information, derive knowledge, and discover truth.

If we are to view the prospects of education in the 1990s based on the track record of the 1980s, it would be easy to resign to a rising tide of despair. Education, after all, is one of the last and best strongholds of thorough-going liberalism. And public education, in particular, has enshrined the tenants of liberalism the way we encase our founding documents in glass in the National Archives.

With the belief system of liberalism as the holy relic of the NEA and most of the teaching colleges and universities that frame the *modus operandi* of education, how can we then realistically chart a positive agenda for conservative values in education for this decade?

Confucius may have said that every one-thousand-mile journey begins with the first step. But, on behalf of Concerned Women for America, I believe it starts with the first three steps.

First Step

We must be effective apologists for the idea that a return to the "basics" in education is the only way we can consistently affirm the mission of education and at the same time not have it self-destruct. Scholars in the education departments who scoff at the "back to basics" mentality claim that the fallacy in the approach rests in our inability to define what the "basics" are and how we ought to teach them.

To the erudite and scholarly among the liberal camp, I then pose this challenge: How about teaching Johnny how to read? A self-governing people are acutely dependent on the skills, the desire, the habit, and the discipline of reading. Without it, the first amendment guarantees of expression and free press are mockeries; without it, representative government becomes a hollow exercise where the most ambitious lead the most ignorant.

Alexis de Tocqueville was right, of course, when he wrote that a democracy becomes a tyranny when the populous becomes happily dependent on the ability of government to fulfill their needs. The youth of today may be willing slaves of tomorrow-slaves to the ten-second sound bite on the evening news, the slick advertising slogan, and the carefully crafted and cleverly manipulated easy-to-read headlines in *The New York Times* or *The Washington Post*.

The literacy problem is illuminated when we realize, as Barbara Tuckman of the Library of Congress has pointed out, that two hundred years ago seven- and eight-year-old readers in America were absorbing incredible kinds and quantities of books. These same youngsters also read aloud and memorized for recitation reams of poetry, great oratories, and classic works of literature. As part of the solution to the illiteracy problem, I suggest the recent report by the Republican Policy Committee titled "Illiteracy: An Incurable Disease or Education Malpractice?" The report recommends a new emphasis on intensive systematic phonics at an early age.

Second Step

We must derail the developmental philosophy of education so prevalent today. This philosophy tells us that the goal of education is not to enhance the learning of our children, but rather direct their total development, especially in areas of social values, morality, and behavior. Somewhere along the line educators started committing intellectual adultery with the behavioral sciences—the result being an almost unilateral, but mistaken, presumption that learning should deal almost exclusively with the affective, emotional plane of the student to the neglect of the cognitive domain.

This emphasis on the emotional needs of children betrays the fundamental mission of education: to arm our children with the tools through which they can process information, derive knowledge, and discover truth. The progeny and offspring of this mistaken philosophy of education are legion: character education, peace education, conflict resolution, family-life education, life skills, suicide education, death education, human growth and development, drug and alcohol instruction, protective behaviors multi-cultural studies, global citizenship, critical thinking skills, children-at-risk classes, self-esteem, and the list goes on.

In short, this philosophy tells us our families are incompetent and our children are sick and in need of therapy. Perhaps Johnny can't read, but public education will certainly help him feel better about it.

When we tell children, even by implication, that cognition is less important than coping, we lead them down the path that motivated Alan Bloom's book, *The Closing of the American Mind*, the path that denies reality of objective right and wrong. There are good books and bad books, but all the coping classes are not going to give our children the tools to distinguish or even care about the difference.

But there is a darker, more sinister problem with this philosophy—its unethical usurpation of the role and moral authority of parents without their knowledge or consent. A few years ago *Education Digest* noted in a survey that the vast percentage of teachers did not welcome more interaction with parents. We must revamp the system so that involved parents will be rewarded, not frustrated; and at the same time we must preserve class time for hard learning rather than making the public schools operate as surrogate parents.

Our daughter experienced this problem when her ninth-grade algebra teacher passed out a worksheet for the students. At the top of the paper were the words, "The Fallout Shelter." The students were asked to choose which of the fourteen people listed on the page would survive in a fallout shelter that would only house seven of the individuals. The group of people were diverse and represented various aspects of society: a black medical student, a Puerto Rican drug dealer, a homosexual, a fundamentalist Christian, etc. My daughter realized that this paper was inappropriate anywhere, but was especially obtuse in a math class. She waited a few moments and then wrote these words on the top of her paper: "I do not feel comfortable with the exercise, and I feel it is an invasion of my privacy. If you have any questions you may call my father at his law office." Fortunately, for our daughter, she knew her rights; but not all children come equipped with their own "built-in" attorney.

Third Step

This step involves the reversal of another troublesome trend: the increasing politicalization of the classroom by liberals. Social studies is a key area where classrooms have been turned into political laboratories. One current theory, "critical pedagogy," which originated from Brazilian educator Paulo Friere and is now in vogue in American schools, clearly aims at engaging students in experiences that implicitly criticize the status quo and, with it, the capitalist system. In one school in Oregon, the class was used to force the military off a public school campus when it attempted to administer an armed service vocational aptitude test.

Current social studies, under a National Education Association-dominated system, use a "global
studies" approach where, rather than stressing the
distinctions between nations, cultures, and land
areas, now stress the supposed web of interdepend-
ence between all peoples and all nations. As a result,
American history and heritage becomes irrelevant.
As an example, it was a tragedy in 1987, during the
bicentennial of our U.S. Constitution, for social studies teachers not to have taught the foundations of our
Constitution, or the social contest that surrounded it,
or the biographies of the delegates who forged it. Instead, many instructed their students to write their
own constitution complete with a new children's bill
of rights. Glasnost notwithstanding, America will
have only a weak and colorless kind of democracy to
export to people across the oceans who are yearning
for freedom if our next generation of Americans has
lost touch with our great heritage of liberty and the
historical facts that undergird our precious freedoms.

As a practical step in dealing with this trend, we
should counteract the National Education Association, which is one of the largest and most effective
unions supporting liberal causes in the country. May
I suggest that we urge those conscientious and committed teachers across the country who still adhere to
that original mission of public education, to utilize
their rights under recent Supreme Court cases and
demand a refund of their NEA dues that go to political lobbying efforts they do not support and for radical resolutions that have little or nothing to do with
educating our children.

As we look at the 1990s and the one-thousand-
mile journey ahead of us, we must be persistent and

committed in this battle for the public school class-room. At stake is nothing less than   the hearts and minds of our children. At stake is nothing less than the ability of our nation's work force to compete in the future world economy. And at stake is nothing less than the competence of our future citizens to run the great engines of American democracy. For the sake of our children and our grandchildren, let us begin the journey today.

FOCUS POINTS

1. What would the "basics" include in your opinion?

2. What should the goal of education be?

3. How can you encourage a teacher you know to be aware of politicalization in the classroom?

4. Do you know a public official who might appreciate this paragraph?

In short, this philosophy tells us our families are incompetent and our children are sick and in need of therapy. Perhaps Johnny can't read, but public education will certainly help him feel better about it.

17

ARE EDUCATORS LEADING OUR CHILDREN DOWN THE ROCKY PATH OF SELF-ESTEEM DEVELOPMENT?

No one is served by an educational approach which seizes the clear responsibilities of parents and assigns it to public school teachers.

J ust about the time parents breathe a sigh of relief—innocently thinking that they have dealt with all the nonacademic instruction now occurring in our public school classrooms—it seems as though another "innovative" program raises its ugly head. The ground breaker for nonacademic instruction was sex education. Since then we have watched programs of all genres enter our public school system—everything from death and dying education to "just say no" drug programs.

The newest programs to gain notoriety, although they have been in existence for quite some time, are ones that purport to assist children in developing positive "self-concepts" or self-esteem. It is no longer vogue for administrators to assume most children are emotionally healthy and simply instruct teachers and guidance counselors to address problem cases on an individual basis. The contemporary approach is to initiate programs—under the watchword of prevention–that establish a type of collective classroom counseling where guidance counselors meet with every class once a month, or teachers take a workshop course and devote a period of time each month to enhancing their students' self-esteem.

One such program currently used in many school districts across this country is Developing an Understanding of Self and Others (DUSO).

What Is DUSO?

According to the authors, "DUSO-1(R) encourages children to develop positive self-images, to become aware of the relationship between themselves and other people, and to recognize their own needs and goals." The program is organized into forty-one goals with a sequence of activities related to each objective. The emphasis of this program is on a child's response to the activities. DUSO emphasizes the students' feelings.

Before discussing the problem areas in this particular approach, it is important to note the primary problem with every self-esteem program designed for the public school classroom. The fundamental difficulty is that classrooms are not the forum for this type of development. Public school teachers cannot become surrogate parents. Assisting a child in developing a healthy sense of self-esteem is an appropriate objective, but it is the business of families, not public school classrooms.

This is not to say that teachers should not recognize what builds and destroys self-esteem. On the contrary, they should be educated in this regard, but only in relation to how they can better handle academic or behavior problems that may arise in the course of a day. Public schools have no business experimenting with programs that require teachers to wear the hat of a part-time clinician or therapist.

Placing this burden on educators is neither fair to them nor the students. It cannot be stated strongly enough: No one is served by an approach that seizes the clear responsibility of parents and assigns it to public school teachers.

Incorporated in this flawed approach is also a tacit commentary on the abilities of parents to raise their children. The assumption seems to be that this collective approach is necessary because parents are failing in their efforts to turn out emotionally healthy children. It is an eve more horrid commentary when one realizes that, given the poor track record of public schools in teaching academics, many child development professionals still must believe that the schools can do a better job of instilling self-esteem than parents.

As with any similar approach, the authors of DUSO justify the use of this program by explaining that for education to be successful, it must address the "whole child." Since DUSO-1(R) is for children of preschool, kindergarten, first and second grades, the introduction states, "Elementary education, by virtue of its objectives, must plan for the development of the whole child." The introduction goes on to quote from a book by the program's authors which states, "Instructors who do not get in touch with the whole being of students will not be able to meet the challenges of education and are destined to fail." Thus, the objective of DUSO is to provide a forum in which the teacher can get in touch with the "whole" student.

How Does That Make You Feel?

Toward the end, DUSO's activities focus on addressing specific affective goals. For each goal, there is an illustrated story, a song, a guided fantasy, a dramatic play activity, and curriculum-related activities. The activities deal with real-life situations that are designed to inspire children to share their feelings.

The rules for the discussion that ensures after each activity are as follows:

1. Think Together;

2. Raise Your Hand;

3. Listen Carefully;

4. Don't Clam Up;

5. Stick to the Point.

The teacher is instructed that the "responsibility for group leadership is shared with all members of the group. . . . There is no single, 'correct' answer to the discussion questions. . . . Lecturing, criticizing, monopolizing, and evaluating are ineffective discussion procedures."

So the stage is set. The students are to discuss activities that deal with their feelings about sensitive ares of self-esteem while the teacher is prohibited from guiding the discussion or evaluating the appropriateness of the responses. To add insult to injury, the student who would rather not share his feelings in this otherwise free-for-all atmosphere is instructed, "Don't clam up."

Every activity in this program (except the songs) serves as a catalyst for promoting discussion about the feelings of the students on specific situations that either build or erode one's self-esteem. Each story, problem situation, guided fantasy, feeling word activity, or dramatic play scenario is followed by a series of questions. The initial questions usually deal with the factual context of the story or activity. But the second or sometimes third tier of questions asks children to relate the situation to personal experiences.

Immediately upon entering these secondary tiers, children move from learning in the third person to learning in the first person through the sharing of personal experiences. Some examples of the probing questions asked are: "Have you ever wanted to do something you knew was wrong?" "Have you ever wanted to do something you knew was wrong?" "Have you ever felt left out?" " Has anyone ever told you to go away because you were different in some way?" "What are some things you are afraid of?" Each of these questions is followed by the standard, "How does that make you feel?"

With so much emphasis on personal feelings, it would be virtually impossible for children not to conclude that every action they take in life revolves around their feelings. Since the teachers are not to offer any guidance, the activities basically set up an environment in which the child's notions of good and bad are supreme. Many of the stories add to this misconception by portraying parents as fellow characters rather than as authority figures.

The fact that there are no single "correct" answers in any of the situations could also lead a child to believe that the only absolute is the majority opinion of the class on that particular day. What a tremendous burden to place on a group of four-, five-, or six-year olds.

Guided Fantasies

The guided fantasies warrant some individual discussion for reasons other than their use as "probing" activities. These exercises carry a greater inherent danger in that they mirror a technique in Eastern religions designed to meet one's spirit guide. Shamans, mediums, witches, and other occultists have employed this technique of guided imagery/visualization for centuries in their quest to gain greater "knowledge" or to live on "higher levels of consciousness."

DUSO's guided fantasies instruct children to lie on the floor on their backs, or sit at tables with enough room to put their heads down. The teacher then plays a tape that leads them through a series of relaxation exercises (another technique of Eastern origin). In the background, the students hear futuristic music with waves rhythmically crashing on the beach. At the end of the tape, the voice tells them,

"Now we're in Aquatron. Imagine you're floating free and relaxed, and let your mind wander." The first guided fantasy card introduces the imaginary guides, Sophie the Sea Otter and Duso the Dolphin. Before the tape is played, Sophie explains to the children that she is going to take them to a secret place called Aquatron where she, Duso, and the other underwater friends sometimes go. She goes on to explain that "what makes Aquatron so secret is that it's inside ourselves." The tape is then played and the children float through Aquatron.

Now, only the authors know for certain whether this technique was meant to introduce the technique of meditation and whether Duso and Sophie are intended to be some sort of spiritual entities. But, regardless of the authors' intentions, parents must recognize that these exercises closely resemble techniques of Eastern mysticism, which teach that divinity lies within each individual as he or she learns to live on higher planes.

Furthermore, no good can come from activities that implicitly teach our children to go within themselves for a safe haven in which to think through the answers to life's questions. Children need the instruction of their parents. Exercises that foster in children a false sense of security about their ability to handle serious hurts or fears without parental guidance are injurious at best.

Some examples of the guided fantasies are as follows:

- Sophie the Sea Otter takes the children to Aquatron where they imagine that "we're doing anything we want to do." Several of these fantasies focus on personal freedom.

- Guided Fantasy Card 6 has Sophie take children on a fantasy where they relive a situation in which someone was unkind to them. After the fantasy, they are to participate in a discussion about the incident. Imagine the potential about the incident. Imagine the potential for privacy invasion during this discussion.

- Guided Fantasy Card 34 takes children on a trip through a dark cave with Duso. After discussing the initial fears of exploring a dark cave, children are asked, "What are some things that you are sometimes afraid might happen?" Depending upon what a child is going through at that particular time (e.g., parents' potential divorce), this question can be a risky one to ask of vulnerable children.

Despite the authors' claims that the DUSO program has yielded impressive results, children would benefit most if public schools would return their attention to academics and leave parenting responsibilities to parents. Our tax dollars are to be used for instruction in the three Rs, not the reorganization of public school classrooms into "therapeutic" encounter groups.

FOCUS POINTS

1. If you find that your school system is using DUSO or a similar program, talk with the teacher(s) and guidance counselors and look at the program. Do not enter the school making accusations. The harmful aspects of these programs can be subtle—so

subtle, in fact, that they can be used by teachers who would never knowingly introduce your children to probing activities or Eastern religion techniques.

2. This chapter discussed the problems with DUSO-1(R). There are other versions of DUSO that we have not yet researched. Parents need to check into what their child's school district is using before assuming the worst.

   Also recognize that we concentrated on the negative points. That does not mean that every activity contained in this program is detrimental. There are some perfectly harmless activities that teach admirable qualities such as patience and cooperation.

3. Above all, try to develop a working relationship with school administrators and teachers, not an antagonistic one. Do not make blanket judgments about programs or curricula without having viewed it for yourself. This chapter is designed to alert you to the use of certain techniques and philosophies. You have the responsibility to review the materials firsthand. As the primary educators of children, parents who choose the public schools must accept the responsibility for remaining informed on course content. No individual or organization can do this for you.

18

EXPERTS PINPOINT HARMFUL EFFECTS OF ROCK MUSIC

Elaine Lussier

The music of one generation seldom appeals to those who grew up in an earlier time. Grandparents of today's young people, who jitterbugged to Benny Goodman's swing, usually did not enjoy Elvis or understand the socially oriented songs of Peter, Paul, and Mary. Therefore it's not surprising that today's rock music is ignored—if that's possible—by parents of current teenagers. However, there's a big difference between Glenn Miller or Joan Baez and the heavy metal group your son or daughter wanted to hear in concert last week. Read this and be prepared to take action.

I t's been said thoughts produce actions, actions produce habits, and habits shape character. Due in a large part to the music kids listen to, the thoughts of America's teens are filled with violence, hate, and pornographic images. In the battle for the minds of America's teens, Christian values are losing.

A recent symposium sponsored by the Parents Music Resource Center focused attention on the harmful effects of rock and roll music on America's young people. Experts gathered to analyze and educate citizens about the realities of the culture of rock music, especially heavy metal. Other sponsoring groups included the American Academy of Pediatrics, the National Mental Health Association, and the Youth Suicide National Center.

Heavy metal rock music is a nonbeneficial form of music with a large teen audience. Although its roots are in rock and roll music, both its music and message are a far cry from the Beatles' innocent "I Want to Hold Your Hand." Today groups like Motley Crue, the Beastie Boys, Iron Maiden, Poison, 2 Live Crew, and AC/DC produce noise-like music with lyrics about violence, sex, drugs, hate, and rebellion.

Experts from the medical, music, law enforcement, and religious communities discussed sensitive issues such as suicide, the harmful physical effects of loud music, drug and alcohol abuse, and occultism. As a forum to educate and motivate, audience members were challenged to be the solution to the harmful effects of the powerful medium of rock and roll music.

At the same time parents are trying to raise kids, educate and support them, the entertainment industry is providing a steady diet of junk food that undermines the teaching of parents and society. "Hard-rock music helps change the values of young people," said Dr. Robert S. Demski, president of the Texas Society of Child and Adolescent Psychiatry. "Kids hear songs over and over and are desensitized to violence, sex, prostitution, and drugs."

He cited a 1960 study that found parents were the group most admired by young people. However, a similar study taken in 1980 found the number-one influence on young people to be friends. Other significant influences mentioned were TV, radio, and records.

What the music amounts to is "commercials for alcohol, sex, or violence against girls," Demski said. He showed various record covers and photos of heavy metal groups. In many of the photos alcohol was displayed. Many of the covers had sexually suggestive pictures or titles. "Much of the music promotes antifamily themes, occult practices, sex, violence, and degradation of women," Demski said.

In the late 1970s and 1980s, kids began listening to punk and heavy-metal music and attending concerts by performers who do sexually explicit or violent acts. At best, many performers condone the use of drugs and alcohol. Occult symbols and practices are used on album covers and mentioned in song. The result of this has been a generation with the highest suicide rate ever, larger numbers of kids using drugs and alcohol, and lower scholastic test scores.

Jevon Thompson, former professional musician, summed up the situation saying, "Alcohol and drugs are found at a rock concert. There will never be a divorce between drugs, alcohol, and rock and roll because they stand to gain by being together."

The theme of caring for our children was a common one. "Each generation has had to care for its kids; some generations have done well," said Dr. Donald Ian Macdonald, administrator of the Alcohol, Drug Abuse, and Mental Health Administration. Our present generation of kids are "doing poorly," Macdonald said. "Young people ages fifteen to twenty-four are dying in accidents, suicide, and homicide." Dr. Macdonald mentioned three possible reasons: negative societal changes, undermining of families and parents, and little hope for families and kids.

In our society, "kids' rights" have greatly increased. "We now have latch-key kids, less family ties and responsibilities. These rights have come at the expense of the parent's ability to guide and protect," Macdonald said.

On the issue of the declining influence of family on teens, Macdonald said parents have turned over the raising of kids to professionals—teachers, counselors, doctors, clergy. "And now they're saying, 'You goofed and we want them back.' " Parents were told music was a part of the culture of the kids and they were not smart enough to understand it, Macdonald explained. "Still others said, 'Anyone can raise kids; mothers need to do things worthwhile and creative,' " Macdonald said.

Dr. Paul King, medical director of adolescent programs at the Charter Lakeside Hospital works with chemically dependent kids, many of whom "love heavy-metal music," he said.

Dr. King showed copies of artwork done by kids in treatment. One picture showed a mother being beheaded by figures in black hooded robes. He analyzed it by saying, "Kids run over their mothers who represent the bulwark in the home." The mother represents values learned at home, he explained. "Most of these kids have learned values but they lose them because the primary person [mother] has become too weak to keep the values going. She may be weakened because she is working, or because she has an alcohol-dependent husband to care for, or because she wants to give her kids everything they want." Kids from this kind of home are open to the world of "sex, drugs, and rock and roll," Dr. King said.

The bottom line of the rock music industry is money, said Jevon Thompson. "When you control money, you control people." He suggested parents teach their kids to be wise consumers. Thompson's advice was, "If you don't like something, stop paying for it." He predicted that until concerned parents and citizens "get down to the money issue" things won't change.

Thompson recommended teaching kids about being wise consumers and the harmful effects of drugs and alcohol when they are in the sixth grade, a time when "innocence and intelligence are in one body."

Suicide among teens has reached epidemic proportions in the United States. Dr. Macdonald works with suicidal kids. Many of these kids are not depressed; they just have "no hope." Hope gives you reason for living tomorrow, deferring gratification, he said. "Kids need to deal with life when things are not going well. Also our kids need a sense of future, values, God, hope—something to make life worth continuing," he said.

"The way to reach young people is not by saying the music's not good, but by reaching out and saying 'You look like you hurt.' "

Dr. Demski said that in relation to suicidal kids "this [the music] is not helping them—it's adding to the problem."

The teen years are often an awkward, rebellious time for young people. They don't feel like they belong with either children or adults; they're looking for some place to fit in. Too often these kids turn to drugs, alcohol, and heavy-metal music. "Kids identify with the power of evil seen in heavy-metal music. It makes them feel big," Dr. King said.

"This sense of power is important to teens. Drugs feel powerful; heavy metal is powerful—we cannot deny it. As time passes, these kids build a wall of hate which the music helps solidify," he said. "Parents must take the power back into their own hands." Once kids get into treatment they are stripped of the drugs and the metal music and become kids again—"insecure and fearful," King said.

Many of the kids who delve into the drug culture and heavy-metal music get interested in the occult and Satan worship. Many of the groups use satanic symbols such as the pentagram or the number 666 on their record covers and in their lyrics. Many of the crimes committed by teens have occultish overtones, said Dale Griffis, a veteran police officer. "Kids may do occultish things as a stunt; but once they get in, it's difficult to get out," he said. "Not one case I've worked with that included traditional occult symbols has there been no sign of drug use," Griffis said.

Occult-inspired games like Dungeons and Dragons have also caught the fancy of teens, said Pat Pulling, founder and director of Bothered About Dungeons and Dragons (BADD). Satanic rituals subtly included in fantasy games "help seduce kids into the occult." Kids often get involved out of curiosity, rebellion against parents and the world. Often young people are recruited into occult groups at rock concerts, she said.

"If kids play it [Dungeons and Dragons] on an obsessive basis, they want to act it out," Pulling said. Some of the games call for behavior like insanity, homicidal insanity, and casting of spells. The danger in these games is that abnormal behavior is "normal in their fantasy world."

To help kids involved in devil worship, Pulling recommended educating people and "showing kids that we still love them."

Ken Wooden, president of the National Coalition for Children's Justice said the "purpose of satanists is to perform evil." He said the "philosophical" messages pumped in heavy-metal songs "are messing up the heads of good, solid kids."

"I believe we can whip them," Wooden said. "Get parents together, share information, get over the bizarre factor," he said. "We can lick the record industry and help people from sliding down the escalator of decadence."

FOCUS POINTS

1. What can be done? For a starter you might read *Raising PG Kids in an X-Rated Society* by Tipper Gore, wife of Senator Albert

Gore, Jr., of Tennessee (Nashville, Abingdon Press, 1987). Its Appendix A details how two cities, Memphis, TN, and San Antonio, TX, have taken action at the grassroots level. Its Appendix B lists a comprehensive Media Action and Resource Agency Directory.

2. Do you really *know* what your child listens to? Find out.

3. Is there evidence of satanic cults in your area? Check with your police department; their youth guidance division might welcome help and encouragement.

4. Are there groups in your area already active in working to require labeling of recordings or to keep away the more bizarre groups?

5. How about a newspaper series detailing harmful effects?

6. As Ken Wooden said, "Get parents together, share information."

7. What can you do?

19

DANGERS OF HOLLYWOOD ENVIRONMENTALISM

Joseph Farah

Can subtle messages about the environment on television hits like "The Cosby Show" impact the way Americans think? If so, what other propaganda is Hollywood feeding us?

With unanimity of purpose, Hollywood's top executives have now formally committed themselves to promoting the environmentalist agenda through entertainment programming.

While most of the nation—and an even higher percentage of Californians—was absorbed by TV news coverage of the massive and tragic earthquake in San Francisco on October 17, 1989, some of the biggest honchos in Hollywood were discussing the industry's role in protecting the environment.

Despite the natural disaster that occurred that evening, some 225 film and TV executives, producers, and writers showed up at Lorimar Studios to hear how they could help stop global warming, ozone depletion, and various forms of environmental pollution.

"How difficult it is to live with nature when nature provides the kinds of tragedies that we can't do anything about," said Norman Lear, president of Act III Communications, in his opening remarks. "How ridiculous it is to be provoking nature to deal us even greater tragedies than what we see on TV in San Francisco."

The meeting and effort by Lear's Environmental Media Association to use television to boost environmental causes was endorsed by the entertainment presidents of all three networks. NBC's Brandon Tartikoff attended the event, but ABC's Robert Iger and CBS's Kim LeMasters were busy dealing with transmission feeds from their San Francisco affiliates.

Lear told those assembled that it is the responsibility of writers and other creative people in TV to "help Americans understand changes needed in behavior and lifestyles." As an example of how TV can raise consciousness, he talked about how his 1970s sitcom "Good Times" featured an episode about the high rate of hypertension in black men and triggered a number of calls from black families interested in learning more about the problem.

As for environmental issues, Lear said, sometimes a single scene—such as a child refusing to use a plastic foam cup—can stimulate discussion about responsible use of products.

"We are capable of having an enormous impact on American families," said Lear. When Bill Cosby is shown recycling his garbage, it will set an example for the nation, he explained.

But is that all Lear and his colleagues have in mind? Will the proselytizing end with pleas for recycling and consumer responsibility? Or, as recent history has shown with other causes, will the environment be hijacked as an issue to promote a more controversial agenda?

John Rich, an executive producer of "MacGyver," boasted at the meeting co-sponsored by Lear's EMA and the Writer's Guild of America that recent episodes of his show dealt with dangerous leaks at nuclear power plants.

"There are not enough people aware of these problems," said Rich. "That's why we can be very useful . . . to penetrate the consciousness of the entire community. I think we have a tremendous responsibility and capability to alter more people, especially kids."

Another speaker demonstrated that the real purpose of introducing such topics into entertainment shows has nothing to do with education and everything to do with programming the minds of viewers. Lauren McMahon, executive director of EMA, said that on a recent episode of "thirtysomething," a babysitter mentioned ozone depletion and the evils of pesticides.

"Certain words like 'ozone' and 'greenhouse' can be integrated into the dialogue," McMahon explained. "[Characters] can make a reference without always needing a speech."

Get the picture? TV will condition its viewers with buzzwords. That's how America's environmental consciousness will be raised.

Meanwhile, environmental scientist Michael Oppenheimer preached to the choir about the destruction of the rain forests, the growing toxic waste problem, as well as ozone depletion and global warming. And though he said that individual consumer responsibility is important in the effort to save the planet, he also made it clear that there is an important political aspect to the fight.

"The big message is this is not a year of leadership in government," he said. "But if anything is going to happen, it has to start at the bottom, through mass communication."

So there you have it. The real aim of Lear's EMA and other allied groups promoting environmentalism in the media is to affect public policy. Media manipulation of the general populace is merely a tool for implementing a political agenda.

It is also abundantly clear that there is much more to this agenda than such admirable ideas as advocating recycling and consumer responsibility with toxic substances. There is a strong antinuclear strain to the rhetoric. There is also what could easily be interpreted as an anticorporate tendency, since so many of the pollution-related problems introduced into TV programs are blamed on stereotypical greedy businessmen.

It's funny how the same people who claim excessive sex and violence on television has no effect on viewers now admit that even passing, subtle messages about the environment will have a profound impact on the national consciousness.

The goals of TV environmentalists are to elect liberal politicians, encourage government intrusion into every facet of our lives, dismantle nuclear power plants, and handcuff developers and businesses.

While everyone favors a cleaner, more healthier environment, not all of us think these are the solutions. That's why it is inappropriate and morally reprehensible for TV's elite to conspire to promote their own narrow ideas on the public's airwaves.

FOCUS POINTS

1. How does the TV industry plan to promote environmentalism?

2. What is the irony of the plan?

3. What could be considered a hidden agenda?

4. Be on the alert for this type of propaganda and develop strategies to combat its effects within your family.

20

PORNOGRAPHY WARS

This article, which appeared in Concerned Women for America *in October 1987, is still germane and should be read as an entity with the following article that appeared in the June 1988 issue. The war against pornography is far from won, even though many people throughout the United States have taken action as outlined here and some legislation has been passed by Congress.*

T he people of the United States are fed up with the abuse of society and its individual members by pornographers. Polls taken by major polling companies consistently show more than 73 percent of Americans want a crackdown by government officials against unlawful forms of porn.

During the last decade, the organized crime network in the United States has made billions of dollars in profits from the pornographers' traffic in bodies of women and children. Through porn outlets, organized crime continues to launder billions made from prostitution, drugs, illegal gambling, extortion, and other crimes. Countless thousands of women, men, and children have been physically and psychologically destroyed through the effects of pornography. Many homes have been broken and countless crimes of sex and violence have occurred as a result of porn.

In July 1986, great hope for change was generated by the conclusions and recommendations in the final report of Attorney General Edwin Meese's Commission on Pornography. Commissioner Dr. James Dobson and other members announced that the war against pornographers was winnable and that most major interstate obscenity distributors could be put out of business within twenty-four months with an "all-out federal enforcement effort."

The plan to stop the pornographers was simple: the ninety-three U.S. attorneys general only had to enforce the law—statutes already on the books and proven constitutionally sound. In addition, Meese appointed a task force to prosecute cases where U.S. attorneys were unable or unwilling to do their jobs. In the first year of operation, this task force cost seven hundred thousand to eight hundred thousand dollars. The commission also directed the attorney general to create a data center to collect information and to provide training to prosecutors and investigators.

Eighty-nine other recommendations were made for federal, state, and local officials, legislators, and the public. A presentation of the commission's recommendations was made at the 1986 CWA convention.

Public opinion was overwhelmingly in support of the enforcement effort. More than two hundred and fifty thousand persons, including many CWA members, wrote the president and attorney general asking that the plan be followed. As a result of this public support, the recommended task force and data center were created at the U.S. Department of Justice.

What else has happened? Across America citizens responded and a new wave of local prosecutions has occurred. More than a dozen cities, including Fort Lauderdale, Florida, and Oklahoma City, Oklahoma, are now virtually free of illegal pornography sales. A new national spirit has erupted, a spirit that rejects the "pornography ethic" that accepts the marketing of human flesh and indignity by the pornographers. Thousands of merchants have quit selling pornographic magazines and video cassettes.

But, tragically, *on the federal level not nearly enough adult obscenity enforcement has occurred.* Form has succeeded over substance and talk over action. Despite public and private pledges and promises from the president, attorney general, and other administration officials, fewer federal adult obscenity cases have been brought to trial after seven years of the "conservative" Reagan administration than during three years of the "liberal" Carter administration. Federal officials, the vast majority of the ninety-three U.S. attorneys, and Department of Justice (DOJ) prosecutors paid to enforce the obscenity laws have simply not done so.

The criminal division of the United States DOJ employs 363 full-time attorneys; the United States attorneys' offices employ 2,274 full-time attorneys. In 1986, the Justice attorneys were involved with 52,581 cases—23,915 of which ended with convictions. Thousands of the cases prosecuted dealt with minor federal crimes and offenses much less harmful to society and much less profitable to organized crime than obscenity. In that same year only ten individuals were indicted for obscenity violations.

Much of the effort by the U.S. attorneys' offices has been directed toward prosecuting child pornography. Adult obscenity cases are seriously neglected. However, it is a *federal crime* to mail or transport obscene matter across state lines. In every one of the ninety-three federal districts, thousands of violations occur annually with almost no law enforcement intervention.

Federal obscenity laws must be enforced and adult obscene materials must be removed from the marketplace.

The time to remain silent has not yet come. Despite recommendations of the attorney general's commission, few pornographers are prosecuted. During the late 1970s, for example, sixty-six individuals were indicted in only three years. (Most of these sixty-six people were indicted in one Florida case.) During the 1980s—the Reagan years—only thirty-four individuals were indicted in seven years.

What Can You Do?

Members of CWA know that direct action on the local level can have big effects. The issue of pornography threatens the family in every community in America. The following guidelines are included to help you know how to encourage your local U.S. attorney's office to begin acting on the guidelines set forth by the attorney general.

1. Write and call your local U.S. attorney's office. Politely but firmly advise him or her

that you are a citizen and taxpayer in their district, that you are aware of hard-core pornography for sale in the district, and that mail or interstate shipments were likely to have been used to get the material into the district. Tell the official that you want the federal obscenity laws enforced. (Carefully distinguish child pornography and adult obscenity violations issues). If you are in one of the districts where the U.S. attorneys are making an effort to enforce the law (Utah, Virginia, or West Tennessee), commend them and ask them to continue until there are no more violations in the district.

2. Send a copy of your letter to CWA in Washington.

3. Invite your U.S. attorney to attend meetings with your local CWA chapter so you can get to know each other. Using public officials to speak on these matters can help to build a good relationship. Most U.S. attorneys have political or other career ambitions. Let each one know how much the people in his or her district will appreciate law-enforcement efforts against obscenity distribution.

To learn of some of the common excuses used for not prosecuting such cases and for suitable responses, write to CWA for a copy of the new brochure on pornography.

Pornography Cases

The following statistics showing the federal indictments and convictions by U.S. attorneys on pornography were provided to CWA by the U.S. Department of Justice's Pornography Task Force.

Obscenity		
Year	Indicted	Convicted
1978	11	20
1979	1	2
1980	54	1
1981	2	15
1982	7	4
1983	0	2
1984	6	11
1985	19	14
1986	10	9
Child Pornography		
Year	Indicted	Convicted
1983	6	14
1984 (before 5/21)	6	11
1984 (after 5/21)	55	35
1985	126	102
1986	147	106

The Administrative Office of the U.S. courts provided CWA with the following sentencing statistics regarding federal pornography cases between July 1, 1983, and ending June 30, 1986. These are the combined figures for all the U.S. attorney districts.

	Sentences which included imprisonment (some also included probation and/or fines)*	Sentences which did not include imprisonment (probation terms and/or fines only)
Child Pornography	51	37
Obcenity	18	32

* Some of these statistics involving imprisonment also include what is called "split sentences." This means that the imprisonment terms could have been suspended if the defendant paid his fines and/or lived up to the terms of his probation.

Districts Which Have Prosecuted Obscenity Cases, 1984–1986:

District	Number of Cases
Central District of California	1
Northern District of California	1
Southern District of Florida	1
Northern District of Georgia	1
District of Idaho	2
Eastern District of Kentucky	1
Western District of Louisiana	1
District of Massachusetts	1
District of Nebraska	1
Western District of New York	3
Eastern District of North Carolina	1
Western District of North Carolina	1
Northern District of Oklahoma	2
Eastern District of Tennessee	1
Western District of Tennessee	2
Western District of Texas	1
District of Utah	2

Districts Which Have Prosecuted Child Pornography Cases, 1984–1986:

District	Number of Cases
Northern District of Alabama	5
Middle District of Alabama	1
District of Arizona	1
Eastern District of Arkansas	3
Northern District of California	1
Eastern District of California	2
Central District of California	13
Southern District of California	7
District of Colorado	4
District of Connecticut	2
District of Columbia	1
Middle District of Florida	22
Southern District of Florida	3
Northern District of Georgia	3
Middle District of Georgia	4
District of Hawaii	1
Northern District of Illinois	4
Central District of Illinois	2
Southern District of Illinois	2
Northern District of Indiana	3
Southern District of Indiana	6
Eastern District of Kentucky	2
Western District of Kentucky	4
Eastern District of Louisiana	1
Western District of Louisiana	4
District of Maine	1

District	Number of Cases
District of Maryland	9
District of Massachusetts	11
Eastern District of Michigan	2
Western District of Michigan	6
District of Minnesota	2
Southern District of Mississippi	1
Eastern District of Missouri	4
District of Nebraska	1
District of Nevada	1
District of New Jersey	2
Northern District of New York	3
Southern District of New York	5
Eastern District of New York	3
Western District of New York	5
Eastern District of North Carolina	2
Western District of North Carolina	5
Northern District of Ohio	31
Southern District of Ohio	2
Northern District of Oklahoma	15
Western District of Oklahoma	2
District of Oregon	3
Eastern District of Pennsylvania	5
Middle District of Pennsylvania	14
Western District of Pennsylvania	6
Puerto Rico	1
District of Rhode Island	1
District of South Carolina	3
Eastern District of Tennessee	1

District	Number of Cases
Northern District of Texas	4
Southern District of Texas	3
Western District of Texas	1
District of Utah	2
District of Vermont	2
Eastern District of Virginia	10
Northern District of West Virginia	4
Southern District of West Virginia	2
Eastern District of Wisconsin	1

FOCUS POINT

Read the next chapter to see how some skirmishes have been won, even though victory in the war against pornography is clearly not accomplished.

21

WE CAN STOP PORNOGRAPHY IN AMERICA!

Kimberly Parker

*It is always heartening to make progress in a right-
eous campaign against rampant evil. The positive
assertion of the title of this article, which appeared
in the June 1988 issue of* Concerned Women for
America—*we can stop pornography—should serve
as a battle cry to spur us onward to final victory.
This article is a followup to the previous one. An
addendum appears at the end that gives good news
and also a plea not to let the goal of final, uncondi-
tional surrender elude us.*

C learly, the pornography industry has dramatically changed in its scope and deviancy. Cogni-
zant of the colossal changes that have occurred since
the days of nudes posing alone, Attorney General
Edwin Meese formed the Commission on Pornogra-

phy and asked it to "determine the nature, extent, and impact on society of pornography in the United States."

During the summer of 1986, President Ronald Reagan and Attorney General Edwin Meese received the final, extensive report of the Commission on Pornography. This report was the result of an exhaustive fourteen-month study.

Upon receipt of this two-volume report, Attorney General Meese divided it among specific divisions within the Justice Department and requested that each division prepare an analysis of the commission data and report to him in September. After several months of study and preparation, the conclusion reached was that the commission data confirmed the findings of several private and state commission reports indicating that pornography and child exploitation had become a serious problem.

The commission report brought the facts concerning the growth of the pornography industry and its devastating social effects to the forefront. Commission research and personal testimonies at commission hearings confirmed the correlation between the consumption of illegal adult obscenity and sexual crimes such as molestation, rape, and sexual assault. The findings concluded that organized crime controlled the industry and what had been a multimillion dollar business in the early 1970s had exploded into a $7 to $10 billion industry.

Heart-rending testimonies at the commission hearings also clearly indicated that the performers in pornographic films, were, in many instances, the subject of abuse. They were virtually controlled by pimps or "talent scouts" and drugged or violently coerced into performing.

Technological advancements were brought to the forefront. Marketing through computers, dial-a-porn, cable, and satellites dramatically increased the scope of the industry.

The content of the pornography had changed drastically. Obscenity was very different in the 1970s, with the major theme being a nude posing alone. Today, pornographic material depicts much more deviant forms of sexual activity.

After careful study of and several high-level discussions on the commission's findings and recommendations, the attorney general responded by introducing a seven-point initiative to curb the growth in obscenity and child pornography. The centerpiece of the initiative, introduced in October 1986, was the establishment of the Justice Department's National Obscenity Enforcement Unit which has two components: the Obscenity Law Center and the Federal Obscenity Task Force.

The remaining five points to be implemented by the Enforcement Unit are 1) enhanced effort by each U.S. attorney's office, with concentration on international trafficking in child pornography and interstate trafficking in obscenity; 2) enhanced effort by the Organized Crime and Racketeering Strike Forces, in coordination with the new task force, with emphasis on organized criminal enterprises involved in obscenity production and distribution; 3) a legislative package to be introduced in the next session of Congress; 4) coordination with the National Center on Missing and Exploited Children to eliminate the use and exploitation of children in the production of child pornography;

and 5) assistance, in the forms of training and sharing of information, to state and local law enforcement agencies engaged in obscenity prosecutions.

Since the establishment of this federal, state, and local network, there has been a tremendous increase in the number of obscenity and child pornography prosecutions. From 1986 to 1987, child pornography prosecutions rose 80 percent and obscenity prosecutions increased over 800 percent. To date, the enforcement unit has held six national training seminars for assistant U.S. attorneys, the FBI, the Postal Service, customs officers, and the IRS as well as nineteen statewide or regional Law Enforcement Coordinating Committee (LECC) training conferences involving seventeen states and thirty-four districts. In the period of one year, these seminars trained three thousand five hundred key law enforcement and prosecutor personnel.

H. Robert Showers, executive director of the National Obscenity Enforcement Unit, lends insight into the need for a national network to combat the pornography industry. Showers explains, "Defense attorneys had a great clearinghouse and network, while prosecutors and law enforcement had none. The prosecutors needed somewhere that would be a clearinghouse for legal opinions, case law, and federal and state legislation." The Obscenity Law Center performs this function. It provides the resources to assist in investigation and prosecution.

The Federal Obscenity Task Force is charged with planning and implementing the national strategy, a federal, state, and local network. Showers concludes, "A local, state, and federal task force is the only way that a problem like pornography and sexual exploitation is going to be solved. It is too pervasive for any one entity to solve. It has got to be a joint venture."

The comprehensive legislative package proposed by President Reagan and unveiled in November 1987, is the last point in the federal strategy that has yet to be implemented. The Child Protection and Obscenity Enforcement Act will bolster the unprecedented efforts already underway to eliminate child pornography and obscenity and dismantle the criminal organizations producing and disseminating this harmful material.

In reviewing the legislative recommendations of the commission, eleven basic areas of weakness surfaced. This legislative package addresses all eleven areas by either closing loopholes or updating existing legislation to address new technology. A brief summary of the provisions stresses the importance of this legislation to criminal prosecution.

Sexual Exploitation of Children Through Child Pornography Provisions

Use of Computers

Research uncovered a loophole in the 1984 Sexual Exploitation of Children statutes that allows child pornography and related information to pass through computer networks. Anyone with a personal computer and a modem can hook into a nationwide pedophile network without violating federal or state law. Child porn producers and suppliers can tap into this system and receive information ranging from files on the children used to actual pornographic material (laser printer needed).

This provision would expand and strengthen the existing legislation to prohibit the use of computers to advertise, distribute, or receive child pornography and related information.

Buying and Selling of Children

Existing federal statutes prohibit the interstate transportation of children for sexual purposes but do not prohibit a parent or guardian (babysitter or day-care worker) from selling or offering to sell a child for use in the production of pornography. This provision will add such a section to current statutes.

Record-Keeping

The pornography industry is not currently required to keep records on the identity and age of performers. Not requiring this information makes it much easier for producers to use minors. Under this provision, the producers will be required to keep records on all performers and have them readily accessible. It would require the keeping of verifiable records as to the actual age and identity of each performer. If a distributor sells material without a statement concerning the ages and identity of performers or where that information can be obtained, the burden will be on him or her to prove that the performers were indeed adults.

Child Pornography and the RICO Statute

The Racketeer Influenced and Corrupt Organizations (RICO) statute provides strong penalties and the forfeiture of assets for a pattern of racketeering activity in which a criminal organization is involved and the proceeds from the activity are used to further their enterprise. If an organization has committed two or more federal violations (covered in the statute as predicate offenses like murder, kidnapping, gambling, fraud, obscenity, etc.) and is using the money gained to further its enterprise, then the organization can be prosecuted under the RICO statute. However, current law does not include child pornography as a predicate offense. This provision would add child pornography to the RICO statute as a predicate offense.

Obscenity Provisions

Interstate Transportation

Under current law, it is illegal to transport obscene material across state lines, but it is not illegal to possess material that was produced in another state. The loophole is that the truck has to be caught in its travel before you can prosecute. This provision prohibits receipt and the possession of obscene material with intent to sell or transfer it. This section also creates a rebuttable presumption that one who offers to sell or transfer two or more obscene materials or publications is engaged in the business of selling.

Syndicate Busters

These provisions tailor federal law to address the organized crime entities that control 85 to 90 percent of the pornography industry.

Interstate Transportation

This provision would amend the statutes to prohibit the use of a "facility or means" of commerce for obscenity trafficking. It would prohibit the use of federal interstate highways and interstate railroads and also prohibit the use of any means of interstate commerce—motor vehicles, boats, and airplanes. Proof of interstate travel would not be necessary as long as the use of a "facility or means" of interstate commerce can be proven.

Presumption of Interstate Transport

Another major loophole in current law is that proof of the interstate nexus is required. Organized crime entities hinder investigation and avoid prosecution by owning the entire chain from production to sales. This provision provides for a presumption that if material known to have been produced in one state surfaces in another, a jury can presume that the material traveled via interstate commerce. This would also apply to material produced in a foreign country. (Note: Mr. Showers indicated that many cases do not go forward because he cannot prove the actual interstate link.)

Acts Furthering Illegal Activity

This amendment will make illegal any interstate or international activity or communication regarding the furtherance of acts which are illegal under state or federal obscenity and child pornography laws. An example of this activity would be a phone call or mail regarding the shipment of obscene material. This activity would also be a RICO predicate act.

Forfeiture of Assets

This provision would provide for government confiscation of the ill-gotten, illegal assets gained from obscenity trafficking. The drafters of this legislation realize that the only way to shut these operations down is to provide for the forfeiture of their assets. The dismantling of these enterprises requires more than the prosecution and removal of the current management.

Use of Federal Lands

Current law does not apply to the sale or transfer of obscene material on federal property. This provision will make the sale of such material on any federal lands a felony, and the mere possession of child pornography on these lands will itself become a misdemeanor offense.

Electronic Surveillance

The final obscenity provision will allow the opportunity to seek a court order for a wiretap in obscenity prosecutions. Current federal law does not provide for this basic tool of investigators and prosecutors.

Cable and Satellite Television

Current law does not prohibit obscenity on cable and satellite television. Actually, the use of cable and satellite is legal-by-default in this regard. This provision will strengthen federal law to prohibit obscenity on these networks.

Clearly, the need for these provisions indicates the weakness of current federal law. Passage of this legislation will greatly facilitate the prosecution of this multibillion dollar industry. As President Reagan stated in his speech unveiling this legislation, "With this act and the implementation of the attorney general's seven-point plan . . . , this administration is putting the purveyors of obscenity and child pornography on notice: Your industry's days are numbered."

This act currently enjoys a vast amount of bipartisan congressional support with 185 cosponsors in the House and thirty-four in the Senate. However, citizen support is also vital. Call your senators and representative and urge them to support the "Child Protection and Obscenity Enforcement Act." But do not stop there. Boycott, picket, and assist in the passage of local zoning ordinances, and support and encourage prosecutors. Our nation's public health and safety depend upon our commitment to the eradication of this life-threatening industry.

Victory Over Porn and Obscenity

In the fall of 1988, the Child Protection and Obscenity Act finally passed as an amendment to H.R. 5210, the Anti-drug Abuse Act. Senators Thurmond (R-SC) and DeConcini (D-AZ) sponsored the amendment.

Originally proposed by President Reagan in November 1987, the amendment is a result of recommendations made by former Attorney General Meese's Commission on Pornography. Two provisions relating to criminal forfeiture and simple possession of obscene material on federal property (allowed as long as there is no intent to sell) weaken the bill. However, it is a significant victory over those who produce, distribute, and view pornographic and ob-scene materials.

A sample of provisions relating to obscenity in-clude these: prohibits the transmission of obscene ma-terial by cable television or satellite dish; adds obscen-ity offenses to the list of offenses eligible for a federal wiretap; prohibits the use of a facility or means of in-terstate commerce for transporting obscene material; increases the penalty for obscene telephone messages; and prohibits the possession of obscenity on federal lands with the intent to sell. Provisions relating to child pornography include the following: prohibiting the use of computers as a means of advertising or so-liciting child pornography; the buying and selling of children for the purpose of producing child pornogra-phy; and the possession of child pornography on fed-eral lands with the intent to sell.

FOCUS POINT

CWA Prayer/Action Chapters and commu-nity-based citizens' groups should continue to be vigilant in their efforts to halt suspected child pornography activity and distribution of such material. It is important to call or write law enforcement officials and encourage them to enforce these new laws.

22

LEGALIZED DRUGS: THE DESTRUCTION OF A NATION

Beverly LaHaye

*In our fight to protect America's families and re-
store the Judeo-Christian values upon which our
country was founded, we now face a new battle: to
protect our children and our country from the
deadly effects of drugs. Although drug abuse has
already destroyed the lives of countless thousands,
there are those who seek to legitimize these poisons
by legalizing their use.*

National frustration over the war on drugs has
produced calls for a dangerous shift in strategy: stop the war by legalizing heroin, cocaine, PCP,
marijuana, and other deadly drugs.

One can understand the frustration of legalization
advocates. They see growing druglord violence, spreading addiction, and police forces who are frantically

striving in vain to hold back the tidal wave of drug use. Legalization seems like the easy way out.

But the arguments for legalizing drugs seduce with their simplicity: legalized drugs would stop gangland violence by taking the profit out of drugs, and treating drugs as a health issue rather than a crime is more civilized and humane. And after all, prohibition of alcohol from 1918–1933 didn't work either.

Like drugs themselves, these arguments shine with false attractiveness, waiting until one commits to the way of legalization before striking with their bitter bite. Legalization would imprison more people in chemical slavery and lead no one to freedom from the war on drugs.

Prohibition points to one reason why drugs should not be legalized: alcohol and tobacco are legal today partly because their use is deeply ingrained in American culture. Indians introduced early colonists to tobacco, and the colonists learned to drink even earlier while in Europe. Americans had been drinking for centuries before prohibition became law. Prohibition didn't work because it attempted to quickly reverse hundreds of years of behavior.

America has no such long cultural legacy for drugs. Before the 1960s, with the Vietnam War protest movement, consumption of marijuana, cocaine, and heroin were limited to tiny groups of people, usually in urban areas. Widespread drug use in America is at best twenty-years-old, hardly ingrained into the cultural fabric of the nation. To surrender to drugs now would cause these vile substances to become as acceptable as alcohol and tobacco.

Even the foundations of alcohol and tobacco in America shake as science unfolds their many tenors.

American smokers have dropped in number by 37 percent in the last decade, according to former Surgeon General C. Everett Koop. He also reported that tobacco kills three hundred thousand people a year; one hundred and twenty-five thousand people die annually from alcohol. The *Chicago Tribune* in 1984 reported that alcohol is blamed in 64 percent of all murders, 34 percent of all rapes, 30 percent of all suicides, and 60 percent of all child abuse. Alcohol is involved in 53 percent of all fire deaths, 45 percent of all drownings, 55 percent of all arrests nationally, and 37 percent of all admissions to state and county mental hospitals.

Alcohol is also involved in 50 percent of all traffic deaths. Anyone who thinks alcohol is a benign drink should remember the drunk driver from Carroll County, Kentucky, who slammed his pickup truck into a church bus killing twenty-seven people.

It's time we all admit that America would be a lot better off today if prohibition had worked.

Why would Americans even consider embracing the fanciful folly of legalized drugs? If we legalize drugs, will we allow children to shoot heroin and ingest cocaine? Even if only adults can use legalized drugs, do we really want stores springing up called Crack and Smack? What about drivers high on PCP or marijuana who smash into church buses returning from a day at the amusement park? Will they be prosecuted?

Therefore if we concede that legalized drugs must be banned to children, and "high" drivers must be punished as severely as drunk drivers, then we admit that easy access to drugs would be dangerous. But what will happen even with partial legalization of drugs for adults? Americans, young and old, will get the wrong message about drugs. Those who see billboards advertising heroin or hear radio jingles touting marijuana, PCP, cocaine, etc., will pick up this sorrowful lie: drugs aren't so bad; they don't hurt anyone; and they're kind of fun. We encourage what we permit.

Today, more and more Americans are taking the war on drugs seriously. In the past, many snickered behind the backs of those who preached drug abstinence; but as the bondage worsens and spreads, we see change. Many television shows no longer wink at drug use the way they did during the 1960s and 1970s. Maybe this is the beginning of the change in attitude that will turn the tide in the war on drugs.

Certainly the drug war has grown in violence and bribery. But just as legalizing alcohol did not eliminate organized crime, drunk drivers, and alcoholism, neither is legalization of drugs going to solve our drug problems.

America cannot surrender to the malevolent sorcery of drugs or the siren song of legalization. It is capitulation and appeasement, a folly we will later regret. The war on drugs is a fight for our freedom. May we never submit to that yoke of slavery.

FOCUS POINTS

1. Why do some people advocate legalization of drugs?

2. Why did prohibition of alcohol not work?

3. Why does the author say, "We all admit that America would be a lot better off today if prohibition had worked"?

4. What lessons could we learn from the history of the legal use of the drug nicotine?

5. Why would it be dangerous to legalize use of drugs only to adults?

23

LOTTERIES ARE A BAD BET

Jordan Lorence

More and more, state governments are facing a money crunch and are searching for ways to increase income. An easy way to do this, they believe, is through officially sanctioned lotteries. And many people like the idea, thinking participation in such events is exciting and fun. However, there are compelling reasons why lotteries are very bad business.

As states rush to legalize lotteries, few are considering the human devastation and economic corrosion inflicted by lotteries.

On April 7, 1987, Wisconsin became the twenty-ninth state to legalize a lottery. Other states ask voters to decide whether to authorize a lottery. States that already operate lotteries are joining other states to start megalotteries, crossing state lines and forming larger jackpots.

Mounting evidence exposes the illusionary benefits of lotteries and their swelling costs.

Lotteries Raise
Little Tax Revenue

In 1985, the states with active lotteries produced from them on the average only 2.8 percent of their total tax revenues. In other words, lotteries produced only a small portion of all of the tax revenues collected by a state, on the same magnitude as the telephone tax or gas tax. Also, lotteries raise revenues inefficiently. Lottery expenses can gobble up 50 to 75 percent of total proceeds, leaving the state coffers with greatly reduced sums. Anyone who thinks a lottery will significantly reduce his taxes will be greatly disappointed.

Lottery revenues gyrate wildly from year to year in many states, making them unreliable, unstable revenue sources for a state. For example, in 1985, one-third of the operating lotteries reported decreases in net proceeds for the year before. As people tire of lottery games, revenues drop off, and lottery officials must think of new games to shore up revenues. Some lottery officials have proposed video lotteries, similar to arcade games, or piping video lotteries into homes via cable TV.

Lotteries Hurt the Poor

Lotteries are a regressive form of taxation, because they are not based on ability to pay. Therefore, everyone pays the same for a lottery ticket, which impacts the poor more seriously than the rich. Also, poor people play certain types of lottery games (such as the numbers games) out of proportion to their numbers in society. When considering all lottery games, poor people contribute a disproportionate share of total lottery revenues.

Some states dedicate their lottery proceeds to aid education or senior citizens, but this does not necessarily help poor people, because no lottery state dedicates funds to help "the poor." Also, the ends do not justify the means. A state could raise revenue by legalizing heroin sales and dedicate the funds to help education. Public schools might receive extra money, but that doesn't make the revenue source morally acceptable.

Lotteries Encourage
Certain Types of Crime

Lotteries encourage two types of crime: illegal gambling and white collar crime. Citizens in a state, their gambling appetites whetted by lotteries and their greed stimulated by state advertising that "You Could Be a Millionaire," begin to turn to illegal gambling. Some illegal entrepreneurs set up illegal lotteries, using winning numbers from the legal state games to demonstrate the illegal game's honesty. Winners of illegal lotteries have several advantages: they pay no taxes; players of illegal games can get credit; and illegal lotteries offer "numbers runners," people who pick up a person's money and buy an illegal lottery ticket for him.

Lotteries also stimulate white collar crime because legalized gambling creates compulsive gamblers. The compulsive gamblers must eventually lose, because the odds are stacked against them. Therefore the compulsive gamblers turn to embezzlement, theft, writing bad checks, and tax evasion, to get funds to buy more lottery tickets. With compulsive gamblers sapping funds from the economy, everyone loses.

Lotteries Create Compulsive Gamblers

Experts dispute the notion that compulsive gamblers are born and not made. Experts say that the more forms of gambling a state legalizes, the more compulsive gamblers it will create. Five states have established treatment programs to aid compulsive gamblers. Ironically, these states fund the program from gambling revenues.

Compulsive gamblers soon become obsessed with gambling and steal to support their addiction. Experts say that compulsive gamblers affect the lives of ten to seventeen other people. Family members must struggle with the emotional devastation of the compulsive gambler's wasteful and destructive acts. Storeowners struggle with the compulsive gambler's bad checks, and creditors get stuck with the worthless notes he signed (compulsive gamblers languish in debt an average of forty thousand to sixty-two thousand dollars, according to several studies).

Lotteries offer a bogus promise of new tax revenue with no pain. During the 1800s, states abandoned the lotteries that had been popular during the Revolutionary War period because they saw the lotteries' destructive effects. Americans should learn from that lesson in history and turn away from the false hopes and real problems presented by legalized lotteries.

FOCUS POINTS

1. Why do lotteries actually fail to raise hoped for revenues?

2. How do they hurt particular groups of people?

3. If there has been talk about instituting a lottery in your state, check facts and figures with a nearby state that has a lottery. Form a coalition, or join one already formed, to combat the lottery.

4. What Biblical injunctions can you find to reinforce your opposition to lotteries?

24

TO LIVE OR DIE: WHO HAS THE RIGHT TO DECIDE?

Kimberly Parker

Literally millions of words have been written lamenting the infamous Roe v. Wade decision. An equal number have been generated by "marvelous advances" in medical science. Here these two subjects are synthesized and correlated in an effort to "tell it like it is"—a horrifying commentary on our "enlightened" life in the last decade of this century.

January 22, 1973, marks the landmark *Roe v. Wade* decision legalizing abortion on demand. Each year this anniversary is recognized by thousands of Americans as they march on the nation's capital in support of life for the unborn. Others simply reflect upon the infamous decision with disdain.

The Supreme Court's willingness to legislate from the bench, with no thought given to the disastrous

consequences, infuriates both the Christian and conservative communities. Anger over the decision and
its role in shaping our current diminished view of
humanity can be constructive, but only if the anger is
correctly focused.

Undoubtedly, the Supreme Court's 1973 decision
is a keystone in our shift toward a low view of
human life, but it is unjust and counterproductive to
place the sole responsibility for the slaughter of thousands and the inhumanities of the day on the high
court.

As difficult as it may be to admit, the responsibility for the infamous abortion decision and the barba-
rous actions of man during the years since 1973 rest
on the shoulders of the American public. Any efforts
to redirect the blame do not alter the truth. The *Roe v.
Wade* decision directly reflected the death of
America's "Christian consensus."

For generations America was dominated by the
Judeo-Christian ethic. The Bible, the inerrant Word of
God, served as the foundation of our societal framework. The view of human life as sacred and unique
is grounded in the Biblical truth that man is created
in the image of God. Legal restraints based upon this
Judeo-Christian foundation prohibit man from acting
upon his unlimited potential for evil.

However, during the nineteenth century, the cultural consensus began to shift away from Christianity. Today, public opinion rests in the destructive te-
nets of humanism. The Christian consensus has been
replaced by a view that proclaims man as the center
of the universe. Man is considered the "measure of
all things" and answers only to himself. God is irrelevant; self is supreme.

As our foundation crumbles, so does the structure of our society. Christianity provided our societal framework and the basis for our laws. Humanism provides no such structure. On the contrary, its doctrine of "doing what feels good" promotes anarchy and hedonism. Law becomes the result of "averages" and, as Supreme Court Justice Oliver Wendell Holmes, Jr., once said, "Truth is the majority vote of that nation that could lick all others."

Ignoring God's existence also paves the way for humanists to obscure and deny the sanctity of human life. Human existence is considered chance, an accidental encounter of the appropriate genetic material. Without the Christian foundation that establishes man's worth as God's creation, no human life is sacred.

If the accepted view maintains that human life is no longer sacred, on what basis can we evaluate and criticize inhuman actions? And, if the consensus no longer recognizes Biblical absolutes, what is to prohibit the Supreme Court from arbitrarily creating its own absolute, the absolute right to an abortion?

Long before the *Roe v. Wade* decision, proponents of the humanist philosophy were working diligently to shape public attitudes. Abortion became recognized as a compassionate solution to an unfortunate woman's "problem." The media focused the public's mind on worse-case scenarios detailing the atrocities of "back alley" abortions. Illegitimate polls and surveys were used as proof of the public's support for legalized abortion. The result of this campaign was the Supreme Court's arbitrary declaration of a new personal liberty: the right of a woman to kill her unborn baby.

Today we are living in the grisly world prolifers predicted. They cautioned the American public against taking the first step down that slippery slope of moral relativism, but their warnings fell on deaf ears. Sixteen years later, more than twenty-five million babies have been slaughtered, abortion pills are now being prepared for distribution, teenage girls can walk into a clinic and undergo an abortion without their parents' consent, and fathers have lost all rights to participate in the decisions regarding their unborn baby's future.

America's trip down the slippery slope has thrust us into what can only be described as the depths of evil. The late Francis Schaeffer made this observation: "Suddenly we find ourselves in a more consistent but uglier world—more consistent because people are taking their low view of man to its natural conclusion, and uglier because humanity is drastically dehumanized."

Where has the acceptance of this low view of human life taken our society? Where will it end?

Children have suffered the most from America's chosen course of dehumanization. Our most vulnerable Americans are exploited and abused at an ever increasing rate. The drastic rise in child abuse is a perfect example. When abortion advocates argued for the right of a woman to kill her unborn baby, they claimed this personal liberty would decrease the incidence of child abuse. Nothing could have been farther from the truth. In 1972, there were sixty thousand reported cases of abuse. In 1976, just three years after *Roe v. Wade*, there were over half a million reported cases. Today, child abuse is the fifth most frequent cause of death in children. Why? Because the

Supreme Court's decision officially sanctioned the destruction of barriers that for years kept man from acting upon his unlimited capacity for evil.

Sexual abuse and exploitation is just another practice of our decreasing view of humanity. The Christian foundation, upon which this country prospered, established firm standards of sexual conduct. Replacing these absolutes with relativistic standards has allowed and perpetuated travesties such as child pornography and prostitution. Children are no longer viewed as gifts from God but pawns in the hands of self-indulgent adults.

Infanticide is another unthinkable practice that raised its ugly head in the wake of the 1973 decision. When the sanctity-of-life ethic was abandoned, it was replaced with the utilitarian quality-of-life ethic. Being human is no longer an assurance for life. A child has to embody the potential to become a "useful" adult. When a disabled infant is born, the question is not "How do we treat?" but "Should we treat?" Before any life-sustaining care is administered to this newborn, the child's "potential for a meaningful existence" is evaluated.

Just as the medical community led the way in the Nazi holocaust and in America's move toward an impersonal, mechanistic view of the universe, it takes the lead in this controversy as well. In 1976, a group of physicians, bioethicists, professors of theology, philosophy, law, and social work met in Sonoma Valley, California, to discuss the fate of handicapped infants in the intensive care nursery. This group decided that the disabled infant's rights took a back seat to the convenience of the parents and the calculated results of certain cost-benefit analyses. Not only did this group agree unanimously that there were times when a baby should not be resuscitated at birth, but seventeen of the twenty agreed that there were times when a self-sustaining baby could be killed. The conditions of the babies need not be extreme.

Proponents of infanticide draw upon the "advantages" of America's humanistic philosophy and separate "personhood" from "existence." Michael Tooley, a philosopher at Stanford University, explains: "An organism possesses a serious right to life only if it possesses the concept of a self as a continuing subject of experiences and other mental states, and believes that it is itself such a continuing entity." The American Medical Association followed suit and set quality-of-life criteria to assist doctors and parents in making the choice of life or death for an infant.

Just as the Supreme Court supported abortion-on-demand, numerous court decisions have distorted the right of privacy, allowing physicians to withhold nourishment or routine treatment from babies sentenced to death by their parents. Baby Doe, a Down syndrome infant born in 1982, starved to death six days after his birth. It was the first case of infanticide to receive nationwide attention. Infant Doe died because his parents desired his death, the doctor acted upon their request, and two Indiana courts condoned and permitted it.

This case prompted the issuance of federal government regulations prohibiting the denial of fluids and ordinary medical treatment to disabled newborns. Four years after enactment of the Baby Doe amendments to the 1984 Child Abuse and Prevention Act, many prominent members of the medical community continue intense criticism of this "federal intervention."

Another form of barbarism prompted by the abortion-on-demand and infanticide rhetoric is the harvesting of tissues and organs from aborted and newborn babies. After all, knowing that a baby's tissues or organs are going to help another individual should certainly make such a difficult but "necessary" decision easier.

In December 1985, the first successful fetal tissue transplant in humans occurred. Fetal pancreatic tissues from aborted babies were transplanted into the body of a diabetic adult.

Surgeons at Loma Linda Medical Center in California performed the first successful organ transplant in October 1987. The heart of Baby Gabrielle, a newborn pronounced brain dead in Canada and shipped to Loma Linda, was transplanted into another Canadian infant. Baby Gabrielle was an anencephalic child with only part of her brain functioning. Anencephalies have a brain stem, which controls the basic life functions, but lack the upper part of the brain which controls the thinking processes.

Currently, the legal definitions of death prohibit doctors from cutting into live babies to retrieve organs, but some desperately want to remove organs from *living* anencephalic children. Their efforts are now directed at redefining "death" to allow such exploitation.

Dr. Bernard Nathanson, formerly a leading abortionist and now an activist in the prolife movement, predicts a ghastly future if this type of high-tech medical outrage is allowed to continue. These loathsome predictions include "withholding of treatment

of extremely premature babies in order to assure
their death and the harvesting of their organs, 'special arrangements' worked out between transplant
surgeons and companies marketing tissues, exploitation of Third World women as organ farms, and
kickbacks to the companies in return for the referral
of the surgeons' names to the purchasers of organs."

Euthanasia is the final utilitarian practice to ride
the coattails of the abortion decision. Joseph Fletcher,
an Episcopal priest and founder of the Right to Die
Society explains, "If we are morally obliged to put an
end to a pregnancy when an amniocentesis reveals a
terribly defective fetus, we are equally obliged to put
an end to a patient's hopeless misery when a brain
scan reveals that a patient with cancer has advanced
brain metastases."

Rita Marker, director of the International Anti-Euthanasia Task Force says that bills to legalize the killing of patients by lethal injection are being considered by the California and Hawaii legislatures and
are slated for introduction in every state. Predictably,
the courts have frequently sanctioned a person's
right to die and allowed family members to make decisions in an incompetent patient's behalf.

If advocates of the right-to-die philosophy are
successful in desensitizing the American public,
many have predicted that in short order the "right to
die" will become "the duty to die."

Clearly, our response to these atrocities should be
anger, but our anger must incite us to action. If we
only criticize and do not act, then we become part of
the problem. Surgeon General C. Everett Koop draws
his own parallel with the abortion battle in a desper-
ate attempt to stir the consciousness of America. He

asserts, "The Christian public was caught napping by abortion and infanticide. It took twelve years for the number of crisis pregnancy centers to equal the number of abortion clinics. Here we are at the threshold of euthanasia, and my plea is let's move faster than we did on abortion."

America's battle lines have been drawn. Choices need to be made—choices that will shape our future. We have witnessed firsthand the disastrous results of complacency and inaction. Stemming the tide of total destruction demands nothing less than total commitment to the restoration of this nation's Judeo-Christian consensus.

FOCUS POINTS

1. Why does the author believe "the responsibility for the infamous abortion decision . . . rests on the shoulders of the American public"?

2. What did Chief Justice Oliver Wendell Holmes, Jr., mean by "Truth is the majority vote of that nation that could lick all others"?

3. What are the direct results of the *Roe v. Wade* decision in respect to (a) child abuse, (b) infanticide, (c) harvesting of tissues, (d) euthanasia?

4. You may be appalled by the revelations presented here, but *believing* is only the first step before *doing* something about an evil.

What can you do? One possibility is to compile a notebook of actual examples, gleaned from newspapers and magazines, to serve as a resource file. What can you do with this file? Remember the longest journey starts with the first step and one candle can be the source for a thousand points of light.

25

EUTHANASIA: THE LAST PRO-CHOICE FRONTIER

Rita Marker*

Euthanasia, the act of killing an individual for reasons considered to be merciful, is totally contrary to God's law and the well-being of society. However, a right-to-die movement is sweeping the country, and it is likely the pattern of the abortion movement will be repeated if euthanasia is legalized: millions will be killed.

S ally was seventeen years old and a senior in high school. She worked hard at an after-school job to earn money for college. Sally put all her hopes and efforts into those college plans. But last week a letter

---

* Director, International Anti-Euthanasia University Steubenville, Steubenville, Ohio

arrived that shattered her dreams. She'd been notified that she hadn't been accepted to the school of
her choice.

Yesterday, when Sally didn't return home from
school or show up at her job, her parents were concerned. Their alarm grew when she didn't come
home all last night. That wasn't like Sally, they
thought. Had she been in an accident? Had she been
abducted? What could have possibly happened?

This morning her parents' questions were answered when a call came from the local "life planning" center—an assisted-suicide clinic offering
counseling about "life choices."

"Mrs. Smith," said the caller, "Sally asked that I
call and let you know she loved you. After carefully
considering her options, she made the decision that
life was meaningless. Mrs. Smith, I need some information from you. Where would you like us to send
her body?"

Sally's story hasn't happened yet. But it could if
the plans of the euthanasia movement succeed. Hard
to believe? Yes. But twenty years ago it would have
been just as difficult to imagine a teenage girl walking into a clinic to end her unborn child's life without her parents knowing about it.

The Supreme Court's infamous *Roe v. Wade* decision made it legal to kill an unborn child until the
moment of birth. In 1973, few people realized just
what an effect that decision would have.

In just fifteen years after that decision, more than
twenty million unborn children were killed. A teenage girl can get an abortion without her parents
knowing she was even considering this "option."
(Parents often don't know about the abortion unless

their daughter suffers complications and someone calls to say, "Your daughter is in the emergency room. Do you have medical insurance?")

Little or no information is given to a woman before an abortion. She is usually unaware of her baby's development or of the help available to have her baby. Rarely is she told about the aftereffects she'll experience. And the so-called "choice" of abortion is often anything but that. Today, when a woman is pregnant, she is *expected to justify having her baby*. Women are under incredible pressure to have abortions.

Killing has become the "preferred solution" to the "problem" of pregnancy. But this "solution" wasn't proposed for the first time in 1973. Long before January 22,1973, pro-abortion opinion makers were working to shape public attitudes. Television programs carried dramatizations about the "compassionate" abortionist who faced jail for "helping" a woman solve her "problem."

Poll and survey results based on biased questions were used as proof of public support for a woman's "right to choose." Stories about "hard cases" such as that of Sherri Finkbine were highlighted by the media. Professional organizations began to endorse the "right" to abortion.

Now the next stage in death advocacy is sweeping the country. The feeling that one has been there before is being experienced by those who have been in the pro-life movement from the days when the public abortion campaigns began in earnest. TV programs feature dramatizations of "friends" or family members who risk jail for "helping" someone take a lethal overdose of drugs.

Polls and surveys with emotionally charged words and misleading phrases are used to document public acceptance of killing in the name of compassion. Explained as the "right-to-die" or "aid-in-dying," such killing has been referred to by its supporters as the "last pro-choice frontier."

Once again, the media focuses on "hard cases." On TV, Robert Young played the role of Roswell Gilbert who "lovingly" shot his wife, Emily, to death. A best-selling book by Betty Rollin, a former ABC newscaster, described how she "helped" her mother commit suicide.

Professional journals have published articles supporting "law reform" which would legalize killing patients by such means as lethal injection or drug overdose. Such laws are being considered for introduction in every state.

If not stopped, where will this death movement lead? It is likely the pattern of the abortion movement will be repeated if euthanasia is legalized: millions will be killed by euthanasia.

Teenagers, like the one mentioned in the beginning of this article, will be able to go to a clinic and obtain assisted suicide or euthanasia without their parents knowing they were considering the "option" of death. Little or no information will be made available to the suicidal person. The person will be unaware of the help available to deal with pain, depression, and other problems.

It is likely that the "right" to choose death will be anything but a choice. The elderly, the chronically ill, and persons with disabilities will be under incredible pressure to "choose" death. They will be expected to request euthanasia or assisted suicide unless they can justify living.

It is of vital importance that concerned citizens realize what is going on in the "right-to-die" movement. Any proposed legislation must be opposed by lawmakers and voters. The power to stop this latest threat to human life is in our hands. How can this be done?

A simple, but effective, four-step program can stop the euthanasia movement's advance in its tracks:

- Recognize that it's a right *and* a responsibility to protect the lives of unborn children and those whose lives are now being placed in jeopardy.

- Pray for guidance and strength in this battle for life.

- Become informed. Know the issues and understand the deceptively compassionate phrases used to sugarcoat the death agenda. Share this information with others by writing letters to the editor or taking the time to phone call-in radio programs. Voice opposition to death as a solution to problems.

- Maintain and treasure a strong family life. The care, love, and support of the most vulnerable in society—whether unborn, handicapped newborn, elderly, disabled, or depressed—can be carried out most effectively by strong, loving families who are willing to reach out to others in need.

FOCUS POINTS

1. What tactics are being used to condition the public to accept the right-to-die as the "last pro-choice frontier"?

2. What groups will be put under pressure to "choose" death?

3. Reread the effective four-step program that can stop the euthanasia movement.

4. Will you commit yourself to following the four-step plan?

26

ADOPTION
FACTSHEET

The alternative of adoption can spare the life of a baby who might have been aborted and can bring joy to couples who desperately want a child. This article answers many questions about adoption, and the Focus Points provide a list of places to receive more information.

The promotion of adoption, a life-giving alternative to abortion, is a major weapon in the pro-life arsenal. However, many pro-lifers don't feel confident in discussing the subject with pro-abortion people or pregnant women.

President Bush recently took a bold step toward promoting adoption by ordering department heads of all federal agencies, including the military, to promote adoption among federal workers. He proposed that the federal government lead the way by providing flexible "adoption-related leave needs of employees" and using agency resources for employees who are considering adoption or whose family members face a crisis pregnancy.

In addition, with the landmark *Webster* decision, many more women will have the choice to consider adoption rather than abortion. Currently only 5 percent of unwed, pregnant teens choose adoption. It's time for that number, and the lives it represents, to increase.

In an effort to educate CWA members, we offer this adoption factsheet with the basics on the subject. This article was prepared by the National Committee for Adoption.

How Many Adoptions Occur In This Country Every Year?

The number of adoptions in the United States climbed steadily throughout the 1950s and 1960s, reaching a peak around 1970. In 1970 there were a total of 89,200 adoptions of unrelated children in the United States. During the 1970s the number of women choosing adoption for their children declined greatly. Today, it is estimated that there are approximately fifty thousand unrelated, domestic adoptions per year in the United States. That figure has been fairly stable through the 1980s, with perhaps some increase since 1982. There has been no national adoption data reporting system since 1975. In 1985, the National Committee For Adoption (NCFA) surveyed the states so that 1982 data is available. NCFA is currently finalizing the data from a survey on 1986 data. Results are available in the *Adoption Factbook II* (see Focus Points at the end of this article).

How Many Teenage Girls Experiencing Unintended Pregnancies Choose Adoption for Their Child?

Only about 5 percent of all teens who experience an unintended pregnancy choose adoption for their child; 40 percent have abortions, 45 percent choose parenting, and the remaining experience miscarriages. It is estimated that approximately 10 percent of teens who carry their babies to term make adoption plans.

Who Can Arrange Adoptions?

Adoptive placements can be made in three ways:

1. Private agencies—those private, nonprofit (voluntary) agencies supported primarily by private funds; these agencies, nonsectarian and sectarian, are licensed by the states;

2. Public agencies—those child-placing agencies that are supported by public funds and administered by public officials;

3. Independently—those placements made without agency involvement; sometimes referred to as private adoptions (not legal in all states).

What Is Involved In a Legal Adoption?

Because state laws govern adoption, laws and procedures will vary. There is no national, uniform adoption law. With this in mind and speaking generally, the legal steps involved in an adoption are these:

1. The birthparent(s) will sign a contract to the adoption or a relinquishment of parental rights. This consent or relinquishment is not legally binding if signed prior to the birth of the child. It generally can be revoked for a period of time (from a few days to several months after the birth). The parental rights of the birthparent(s) are usually terminated in a separate legal proceeding. The biological father of the child generally must be notified of any adoption plan. Procedures for notification of the biological father vary considerably.

2. Separately, the prospective adoptive parents must file a petition to adopt. The court will order a time of supervision; during this time the adoptive parents have custody of the child, but the adoption is not yet finalized. The court may also enter a temporary decree of adoption when the petition is filed. After this time of supervision, often between six months and one year, if the court is satisfied that the adoptive placement is satisfactory, the court will finalize the adoption. The adopted child will then enjoy the exact same legal footing in the family as a biological child.

Are There Children Waiting
To Be Adopted?

There are waiting lists of couples to adopt children in this country. It is estimated that there are at least forty infertile couples who would like to adopt for every baby available. This does not include the large number of fertile couples and single persons who would like to adopt. Babies generally do not wait for families.

It is often more difficult for agencies to recruit minority families for minority babies. Even then, minority babies generally do not wait more than a couple of months. There are waiting lists of couples who would like to adopt infants with Down syndrome and spina bifida. There are also a large number of couples who would like to adopt terminally ill babies, including babies with AIDS. However, there are approximately thirty-six thousand children in the public foster care system who are legally free and waiting for families. These are mostly "special needs" children, who are generally defined as children who are older; members of sibling groups; emotionally or physically disabled; or older kids who are members of a minority group. In many cases there are families who are willing and able to adopt these children; barriers in the system, however, prevent the placement.

Is There Money Available
To Help Parents Who Adopt
These Special Needs Children?

All states have adoption subsidy programs designed to assist parents with the costs of caring for a special needs child. Federal matching funds are available for adoption subsidies for certain eligible children, who are also then eligible for Medicaid coverage.

What Happens to Teens Who Choose Adoption For Their Child?

According to Christine Bachrach's report, "Adoption Plans, Adopted Children, and Adoptive Mothers: United States Data, 1982," women who make adoption plans are less likely to be poor (18 percent) than women who were unmarried at the time of birth and chose to raise their children alone (40 percent). A total of 77 percent of the women who choose adoption for their babies finished high school; only 60 percent of the women graduated who make other choices. Women who choose adoption were more likely to marry subsequently (73 percent), compared to those who were unwed and chose to raise the child alone (51 percent).

A study by Steven McLaughlin corroborates these findings. His data indicates that women who choose adoption:

- are more likely to delay marriage;
- are more likely to be employed and have a higher income;
- are less likely to have a repeat out-of-wedlock pregnancy;
- are less likely to abort subsequent out-of-wedlock pregnancies;

- do not suffer more negative social/psychological consequences than single parents;

- report high satisfaction with their decision about adoption.

What Happens to Children Who Are Adopted?

Bachrach reports that children who are adopted are better off economically than children living with their birthmothers who gave birth out-of-wedlock. Adopted children also have better educated, older mothers. Only 2 percent of adopted children lived in families below the poverty level in 1982 compared with 62 percent of children living with mothers who never married. A study by Marquis and Detweiler found that adopted persons saw themselves as being more in control of their lives than the nonadopted comparison group. They also significantly demonstrated more confidence in their own judgment than the nonadopted group.

FOCUS POINTS

- Bethany Christian Services
  901 Eastern Avenue, NE
  Grand Rapids, MI 49503
  (616) 459-6273

This is one of the largest private adoption agencies in the country. It also operates a crisis pregnancy lifeline at 1-800-BETHANY.

- Family Life Services
  c/o Liberty Godparent Home
  1000 Villa Road
  Lynchburg, VA 24503
  (804) 384-3043

Associated with nearly one thousand agencies for adoption across the nation, it also provides pregnancy counseling and residency. A twenty-four-hour hotline is available at 1-800-LG-CHILD.

- National Committee for Adoption
  1930 17th Street, N.W.
  Washington, D.C. 20009-6207
  (202) 328-1200

NCFA is a nonprofit advocacy group for information on maternity and adoption services. It works with 140 private adoption agencies nationwide. Information packets and publications lists are available, including *Adoption Factbook II*. Pregnant women can call collect (202) 328-8072 for hotline services.

27

WHY FEMINISM NO LONGER SELLS

Beverly LaHaye

This is my credo, a statement of what I believe. I think there are millions like me in America, and our number is growing.

There is a conservative woman emerging on the horizon who has yet to be seen in full strength. During the last decade, conservative women have become activists because they have seen a threat to their home or their family. Women are realizing the truth in the statement "the hand that rocks the cradle rules the world." But many feminist women want to rule the world without rocking the cradle. They want to do away with the cradle but still be rulers over much of the world.

We are told in several places in the Bible how important the family is and about the important role played by women. It is only because that role has

been questioned by the feminist movement that anything has changed.

When the feminist movement failed to recognize
the importance of marriage, the family, the home,
and other God-established institutions, they missed
the greatest asset in building strength in their own
organization.

The feminist movement is not new. Beginning in
the 1800s, unhappy women began to look outside the
traditional framework of marriage and family to find
"fulfillment." In 1840, the French feminist writer
George Sand promoted her brand of socialism in her
writings. George Sand was born Amadine Aurore
Lucie Dupin, but she took a man's name and wore it
as a slogan. She wrote in her socialist philosophy, "I
continue to believe that marriage is one of the most
hateful of institutions. I have no doubt whatever that
when the human race has adapted further toward
rationalities and the love of justice, marriage will be
abolished."

Even Sand, one of the earliest feminist writers, was
talking about abolishing the institution of marriage. In
England, the spotlight fell on Mary Wollstonecraft,
considered the founding mother of the nineteenth-cen-
tury feminist movement. She hated men and marriage,
but not without good reason. Her father was a vulgar
drunkard who regularly beat his wife and terrorized
the six children. Mary became a touchy woman who
scorned a loving home environment.

In the 1800s and early 1900s, feminist demonstrations were instigated by women who did not have a
loving family background, one where men made a
contribution to the home life and family.

Historians in the twentieth century have called Betty Friedan the founding mother of feminism. In her book *The Feminine Mystique,* Friedan says, "The changes necessary to bring about equality were and still are very revolutionary indeed. They involve a sexual revolution for men and women which will restrict all our institutions—child rearing, education, marriage, the family, the architecture of the home." In her earliest writing, Betty Friedan was critical of the structured institutions that have made America strong.

Gloria Steinem is another feminist leader to be reckoned with. She also came from a very chaotic and unstable home. She said, "to think of those who wish to live in equal partnership, we have to abolish and reform the institution of legal marriage."

Many of the same themes in the early feminist writings are still sounded today. These feminists do not see the importance of a good marriage, a solid home life, children being reared by a mother and father. Many people who have been brought up in a strong family with high-quality values cannot identify with the feminist movement.

One of the recurring selling points of the feminist movement is tapping into other people's bitterness toward men and the family. The message they send is antifamily and has been identified with the lesbian movement, which is largely composed of men-haters. In fact, the lesbian movement sponsored a conference in January 1984 that was called the Lesbian Rights Conference. At the conference, lesbian women were trained about their rights and how they could get involved in politics without exposing everything about themselves.

I believe that in all this the feminists went too far. Instead of bringing American women along with them, they began leaving them far behind. Lesbianism is not what American women generally want to represent them and their values.

The desire for healthy relationships with men, marriage, and family living is a natural part of the majority of women. I believe we cannot hide that fact. During the last eight years, for example, the number of women over thirty who have given birth to children has doubled. These women could have had abortions, but they had a baby hunger. Despite attempts by the feminists and the media, the fact remains that women still want to raise a family. When the feminists attempt to deny the hearts of women and lead society to fall in step with them, they begin to lose the interest of women.

Not long ago, I was invited to be a guest on the Sally Jesse Raphael television show. The subject was sperm banks. Although none of the other guests were currently married (one had been previously), they all had a desire to have a baby. The other women interviewed were professionals over thirty. The women on Sally's show all understood that the time was rapidly approaching when they would no longer be able to have babies, and they wanted them. So these women went to the sperm bank. One woman had an infant with her on the show. Another woman had a three-year-old and was planning to have a second child very soon; the third had a young child. None of these women had husbands.

What position did I take? I believe that when God put the family together, He intended there to be a father and a mother. Even in a home where there has been a divorce and the father is no longer present, or in any family with a single parent, the child knows somewhere back in his or her past there has been a father and a mother. But these sperm-bank children do not have that. They go back to their beginning of a mother and a sperm bank.

In the limousine going back to the airport, I got into a discussion with the mother and her three-year-old. This mother had assured us that her child was accepting her beginning very comfortably, was well-adjusted to this new kind of family, and would have no trouble growing up with it all. And then in the car, the child looked at her mother and said, "Do I have a daddy?"

The mother quickly responded, "Well, no. You don't have a dad. I told you about it."

The child said, "Oh, yes, I do. Remember? You said my daddy was a doctor, but he was in a sperm bank." And it is true. The sperm was from a doctor.

This three-year-old was a wise child. After a few moments, the child looked up and said, "Mother, will I ever see my daddy?" The mother looked like she wanted to slap her hand over the child's mouth as if to say, "You said too much." But she said, "Well, of course not. You'll never see your dad."

If that little child is asking such questions at three, what will be her reaction when she is seven or ten or sixteen? I wondered.

In the natural family, God said that there is to be a father and a mother. The urge to have children is a natural one, but women of the 1980s are trying to fulfill their desires without adhering to God's design of marriage.

Concerned Women for America was founded in 1979, but was still very small on the West Coast. I was appointed to the San Diego County Commission on the Status of Women. Twelve of the thirteen commissioners were outspoken feminists. I was the lone traditional woman. Newspapers all over the county talked about my traditional past and the fact that I was the wife of one husband and the mother of four children. That was considered newsworthy.

The discussions that came out of that commission basically were how to deal with children during the day while mothers were working. How many day-care centers can we establish in our county? How many children can they accommodate? How many women can we get into the workplace?

I began to realize these women did not place a very high value on human life. They would come to the commission meetings and casually talk about the number of abortions in the county that month. I began to see the vast difference in the outlook of these women versus conservative women.

Conservative women, on the other hand, put a high value on human life. They fight for the protection of the unborn baby. They want that baby to be born, and they try to give it all the normal home life, love, training, education, and parental guidance possible. Many feminists try to see at how early an age children could be cared for at a day-care center.

We did an evaluation of each day-care center and found that there were centers in San Diego that would accept children at three weeks. That meant only three weeks for a mother to be full-time with her child. I began to see the great advantage traditional motherhood provided in the daily, consistent training in the character of her children. The future of children with a solid value system molded by a caring family is bright.

I believe feminist women lost ground when they focused on themselves rather than the family. I found these women to be totally engulfed with their own selfishness. From the feminists I heard terms such as "my life," "my choice," "my career," "my, my, my." In contrast, conservative women focus on other people; they are givers, not takers. Feminists, basically, are takers. Their outlook is based on "what is best for me, what will benefit me, my job, my body," and so on. Putting it simply, that is the greatest difference between feminist women and conservative women.

CWA's recent project helping the Nicaraguan refugees in Costa Rica was launched in response to real need and in keeping with the conservative ideal of helping others. This is a glorious illustration of giving, not taking. I have seen no evidence of any feminists who have offered to help these poor victims caught in a situation they cannot control. Conservative women were there, reaching out to others, trying to meet their needs.

I think conservative women are moving forward today because they are family-oriented. If there is any truth in that old adage mentioned earlier, "the hand that rocks the cradle rules the world," women who are family-oriented will find out. Children raised in conservative homes are America's greatest asset for the future. Parents have the greatest power in influencing politics, values, and legislation for their children.

We are reminded of this in the Tennessee textbook case. The case is not about book censorship, as was reported by the liberal press. The parents in Tennessee are not against any one book. They are concerned about the overall education of their children. These parents are concerned that their children are not getting the proper education, but are being indoctrinated by a variety of values that are not in keeping with their own. The parents simply asked for a substitute reader to be given to their children. This is not censorship. We dare not ever deny American parents their right to have the final say over their children's well-being, education, and the values of family life.

I travel from border to border, from ocean to ocean, across the United States. I see the difficulties of women who have lost their strength and self-worth. Whenever you remove a woman's high value toward family, marriage, and children, you begin to weaken her feeling of confidence. A woman's greatest self-worth can come in rocking that cradle; in building the lives of other human beings; in helping babies grow up to become children who read and write, begin to develop values and principles, and become teenagers who move into adulthood.

Feminism tears down a woman's feeling of self-worth. There can be no feeling of self-worth in a woman who harbors and displays bitterness and hatred toward the male sex. Feminists may not say they hate men, but their actions speak louder than words. They say that women are superior to men, but one is handicapped if she is born a woman. Feminism continues to sell a confusing message.

Although mothering is an important part of being a conservative women, not all women will be mothers. Many women with grown children are finding a

niche in their communities as successful professionals. Other professional women—career women—
prove you do not have to be feminists to be successful. I think it has been quite a shock to the feminist
movement that many women have risen to success:
Sandra Day O'Connor, Elizabeth Dole, Nancy Kasse-
baum, and a long list of women outside politics.
Many of these women are traditional, married
women who have gone to the top of the ladder. It is
quite shocking to feminists that some of them could
be successful without endorsing the principles of
feminism.

The whole idea of being a conservative woman
builds a woman's self-worth; she has absolutes to
stand on: moral values, the family, the home. She en-
dorses the institution of marriage. This conservative
woman is born to win, not lose.

Part of Concerned Women for America's goals is
to give conservative women the tools to organize and
succeed. Give a woman such important tools as how
to speak publicly, how to work with the media, how
to express herself on the issues, and she begins to put
it all together and make an impact.

I have seen women with the heart to do something and all they need is some help. I have seen
women become successful who have never been involved in the political arena before. We have seen
women who have branched out and are contributors
in their state. Some women have become city council
members, serve on educational boards, and assume
other political roles. These are not feminist women.

A conservative woman's heart is focused on her
family. She needs to influence and test those institutions that affect her family, whether it's the schools
or the government. She even can go a step further to

protect the borders of her country. (This is one of the reasons why CWA is involved in supporting the Freedom Fighters in Nicaragua.) Conservative women become involved because situations like Nicaragua might affect their families and the kind of nation that will be presented to our children and our children's children.

We are born to win. I once heard a story about a man who was walking through the streets of Hong Kong. As he walked down the street, he came to a tattoo shop and looked at the messages and pictures people could choose. One caught his eye. It said "Born to Lose." Nobody, he thought, would ever select that to be tattooed on his flesh. He went inside and talked to the man who owned the tattoo shop. He said, "I'm curious about this tattoo that says 'Born to Lose.' Does anybody really come along and have that tattooed on his chest?" The shopkeeper responded, "Before tattooed on chest, tattooed on mind."

Conservative women need to tattoo on their minds "We are born to win." The hand that rocks the cradle is going to help the rulers of the world. Influence? Yes. Raising up young people that can be good? Absolutely. Giving them strong values, a strong family life? Important. These ideals are on the rise, and I am here to tell you that conservative women are going to win.

FOCUS POINT

To put something down on paper emphasizes it, making it more important. Also, the act of writing requires first that the ideas to be written must be thought out, defined.

Why don't you write your own credo? Start off with "I believe . . ." Then add "I am . . ." (tell what you *are doing* to live up to your beliefs). Finally write "I will . . . " (define your goals for the future).

28

WEYRICH URGES CONSERVATIVES TO GAIN CONTROL OF THE GRASSROOTS

Paul Weyrich

At the CWA convention in September 1988, Paul Weyrich, president of the Free Congress Research and Education Foundation, urged the audience to translate their anger at recent reversals in Washington into action at home. Here are some highlights of his speech.

W hen you talk about the state of the conservative movement—and when I say conservative movement, frankly, I'm really talking about us—the interesting thing that's happened is that the values-related people have overcome the bias against us that occurred ten years ago and have now dominated the conservative movement.

Even institutions that vowed two or three years ago they would never work on social issues have been forced to put on people to work on those social issues. So powerful are we at the grassroots, where the money is, that they have to respond.

But in terms of political influence in this country, we are being written off, incorrectly, because there are a lot more of us than there are of them. And if we ever get our act together, and we organize properly, there is nothing that we can't win, and there is nobody that we can't elect and nobody we can't debate.

The problem is this: some people, I think, confuse the Scriptures. I think that some people misread love for our neighbor, love for our enemies, as capitulation to our opposition. That's not true. Scripture does not tell you to do that. As a matter of fact, if we love these liberals as we must, if we love these apologists for the Soviets as we must, if we love these people who are, despite the terrible pain that it takes to even say it, helping to murder the unborn as we must, then we want what is right for them. And what is right for their immortal souls is to get them out of public policy in this country.

Now, we will never control the situation in Washington, on the Bork case, until we control the situation back home. The reason that we have lost some issues was not in Washington. We delivered the calls and the letters and the lobbying back here. The reason we lost is because those people were active back there. They encountered the senators and the congressmen as they came home for congressional visits, as they went to their town meetings, as they held office hours. The other side was omnipresent, and we were not to be seen. And believe me, the one thing that these people understand is when the threat is real. I'm afraid we have lost the momentum of 1980. We are going to have to go back and take a few of them out and then they will understand again.

Ultimately, of course, we have to begin to recruit people at the state and local level. There are plenty of vacancies at the precinct level in both parties across the country. People need experience. We have about a third of the state legislative races in the country that are practically uncontested. People are running without opponents. That is a horrible situation. We have already, for the next election, about 35 to 40 percent of the Congress who are effectively re-elected because they don't have new opposition. That's a crime. We need to get active at the local level. We need to recruit people. We need to build organizations. We need to put coalitions together. We need to put aside some of our historical and other kinds of differences, and we need to work together at the grassroots level and take control.

Ultimately, we want to take those people that get elected at the local and state levels and we want to get them elected to the federal level and send them to Washington so we have a pool of righteous men. But that will take many years to do. And until that time, we are to work and operate with the system the way it is. And the system the way it is, you've got a bunch of people here who have no principles at all.

My friends, it's just like in battle, just like a war. Because fundamentally, this isn't about Democrats and Republicans, is it? It isn't about conservatives and liberals, is it? It is about right and wrong, and truth and untruth; that's what the battle is. Don't let them tell you, "Well, if it's a Republican, it's all right." If it's a Democrat, that's fine. That's a lot of nonsense. Party labels mean nothing.

We have a saying in diplomacy and war that you never get anything at the negotiating table that you haven't won on the battlefield. And it is the same in politics. We will never get anything back here until we control the territory back there. When we take control of our states and localities, and we can point to mayors and sheriffs and county board members and school board members and state legislators and finally Congressmen, then, we can talk about advancing our agenda in this country and not until then.

It's time to roll up our sleeves and get into the precincts. We've got to tell our fellow Americans, our fellow Christians, our fellow conservatives: "Now is the time to roll up our sleeves and get busy on all this." Because it's going to take time. We're not going to have this happen overnight.

We Christians believe in but one Savior. Why do we think it's a political savior? It's not up to Ronald Reagan; it's up to us. We're the people who have the belief, and believers have power. The devil only has such power as we cede him. He doesn't have any power. So let's get out there and use it for the good of mankind and the political process.

FOCUS POINTS

1. The speaker said, "Now is the time to roll up our sleeves and get busy," at the grassroots level. What specifically does he recommend doing? Make a list.

2. The situation is different in each locality. Beside each action step you listed, suggest a definite target to pursue or objective to try for.

3. Now write down how you think the goals could be achieved.

29

LETTERS TO THE EDITOR EDUCATE PUBLIC, PROVIDE BALANCE

Kathleen Masters

This is good, practical advice on how you can make a difference—and have fun increasing your awareness at the same time.

It's another sunny Saturday afternoon in southern California and a filmmaker, two army colonels, and an encyclopedia salesman are gathering in a friend's home for a weekly support group. The esprit de corps of the three-year-old, one-hundred-member group is strong as they meet to encourage one another and swap information and success stories.

But this is not your typical support group. The members of this eclectic group have carved time out of their crowded schedules not to discuss affection for food or drink, but to discuss their fondness for the written word and for getting their views into newspapers and magazines they feel are often reticent to print conservative opinions.

They are writers not of features and not of news, but of letters to the editor. Their group, the National Writers Network, is a nonpartisan, grassroots organization founded three years ago by Californian Mimi Jaffee with her husband, Sydney, a retired businessman.

"We're an informal, no-frills group that meets for education and kinship," Jaffee said. "We feel that some of the best, most well-informed writers around are people from the conservative perspective, but they often don't have a forum and don't get their viewpoint published."

"We want balance and fair representation in letters to the editor sections, not all conservative letters," Jaffee said, explaining that her group is made up of committed Democrats and Republicans. "The tie that really binds us is our desire to raise awareness about freedom."

"When we get together in a living room, things become alive because there is that passionate commitment to freedom," Jaffee said of the group. "We may not see it in the same way, but we all want to perpetuate and preserve it for the next generation."

Jaffee, a mother of three who calls herself a "citizen-writer" and activist, said she founded the group after several unsuccessful attempts to get her own letters published. "I found bias against my viewpoint, so I started calling people up whose letters appeared and asking questions and swapping information," she said. Those conversations eventually evolved into the letter writers group over which she now presides.

During meetings, members of the group read letters to each other, discuss ideas, share literature, and listen to guest speakers such as editors.

Learning from their collective experience, members of the group now regularly see their letters on the printed page. Jaffee herself admits to writing "hundreds of letters" over the years, and has had letters appear in *Time* and *Vanity Fair* magazines, the *Los Angeles Times,* the *Chicago Tribune,* and numerous other periodicals.

"I'm an inveterate letter writer," Jaffee says of herself. "I believe it's a civilized form of communication, and it's proactive. When you put something in writing, you're asking people to really consider it and respond. That's an advantage to the written word."

For those yearning to see their letters printed, Jaffee advised: abide by the basic requirements laid out by editors and don't be discouraged if your letters do not always get published.

"People who write letters to the editor hungrily search for them to appear and are often disappointed, especially if they're a conservative," Jaffee said. "But people should not be discouraged. They should know that, regardless of whether or not their letter got printed, it had some impact because at least one editor read that letter."

For more impact, Jaffee advises: "Broaden the base of those you send your letter to." She suggests sending it to the reporter who did the original story a writer is commenting on, as well as to the board of trustees or the president of the company. Although the latter probably won't help get a letter printed, it may have a subtle influence on those more conscious of the status quo, she hints.

"A lot of effort goes into these letters, and it's a shame for only one editor to see them. Writers should get their letter into circulation." Jaffee said.

On the mechanics of letter writing, she echoes editors: be brief and know your facts.

"We feel our letter writers are often better informed than reporters, but writers shouldn't look at them as adversaries. A writer should try to provide information that can raise awareness," she said.

Jaffee encourages would-be letter writers not to forget their local papers. "By all means, write to your local papers. They are hungry for letters and will print almost anything. There is not as much competition."

For conservatives looking for impact over the long haul, her advice does not belie her actions: grassroots activism. "The most important thing is to organize locally. The left is expert at forming coalitions and organizing around special interest groups. Conservatives need to pick up some of their techniques."

"We don't have any vainglorious ideas about ourselves, but our small group effectively contributes to raising public awareness," Jaffee said. "That's our little contribution, to gain fair exposure for our ideas."

Is it really worth all the effort? "You bet," Jaffee says. "I have learned from experience that one person can make a difference with a letter."

Jaffee said her group plans to begin publishing a newsletter and welcomes inquiries on how to form a letter writers group. Inquiries may be directed to:

National Writers Network, Box 1552, El Toro, CA 92630.

FOCUS POINT

The blueprint is here. Will you take advantage of it? Try it!

30

CAN ONE PERSON REALLY MAKE A DIFFERENCE?

Jane Chastain

*The answer is yes, one person can make a differ-
ence. Read this to see how.*

A sk not what your country can do for you—ask
what you can do for your country."

Those familiar words, uttered by the youngest
man ever elected president of the United States, are
perhaps even more relevant today than they were in
1961 when John Fitzgerald Kennedy delivered them
in his inaugural address.

What can you do for our country? At the very
least you can be an informed, registered voter.
Maybe that doesn't sound like much to you along-
side the accomplishments of a man like John F. Kennedy, but consider the fact that Kennedy won that
election back in 1960 with a margin of just one-half

vote per precinct. A handful of voters controlled the fate of this president and gave him the opportunity to do something for his country from the highest office in the land.

How important is one vote? Literally a handful of voters have controlled this country time and time again.

One vote was important to Kennedy, but one vote was even more important to Lyndon Baines Johnson, the man who succeeded Kennedy after he was assassinated on November 22, 1963. If just eighty-seven people in Texas had stayed home and had not cast their one vote for Johnson in his race for the Senate against Coke Stevenson in 1948, chances are he would have been stopped on his road to the presidency. That was Johnson's margin of victory. He was given the nickname "Landslide Lyndon" at that time, and that nickname stayed with him until he died in 1973. Lyndon Johnson never forgot the importance of one vote.

An even closer senatorial election occurred in the state of Nevada in 1964. Howard Cannon retained his seat that year by only forty-eight votes.

Grover Cleveland was elected president in 1884 by just a handful of folks in New York. Oh, the other states voted, all right, but just 575 voters in his home state gave him the margin he needed in the electoral college to become our twenty-second president.

As late as 1976, a few people in just two states could have changed the course of our nation's history. If one person in each precinct in Ohio and six in each precinct in Mississippi had voted for Gerald Ford, Jimmy Carter would not have been our thirty-ninth president.

The examples of close-call elections on the state and local level are too numerous to mention, but one of the most dramatic occurred in the state of Massachusetts many years ago. Marcus Morton needed a majority of 51,034 votes to become governor, and that's exactly what he received.

In 1984, in Waterbury, Connecticut, Joan Hartley won her state legislative race by only two votes out of nearly ten thousand cast.

What about congressional races? Remember your congressman is your most important link to Capitol Hill.

In 1984, six house seats in North Carolina were decided by 2 percent or less of the eligible voters.

In 1984, Frank McCloskey was finally declared the winner by four votes in Indiana's eighth Congressional District over Richard McIntyre after several recounts. That same year, Joe Barton made it to the House of Representatives after winning a primary runoff in Texas by only ten votes.

Just think of it—ten votes—that's your vote and nine of your friends. Do you know ten people in your state who didn't vote in the last election for one reason or another? I'll bet you do.

Only 64.1 percent of all eligible to vote in this country are even registered. That means over sixty-two million people have never even bothered to exercise one of their most precious freedoms, a freedom many of our ancestors fought and died for. The sad fact is that only about half of Americans of voting age go to the polls on election day and the percentage of Christian voters is even less.

Why?

The act of casting a ballot is the easy part. It only takes a few minutes of your time. Automation and the number of polling places have virtually cut out the long lines, but casting an informed ballot is another matter.

The sheer number of offices and issues is often mind-boggling, even in a local election. So many people wait until the last minute to look them over, and then quietly retreat, overwhelmed. How can you avoid being overwhelmed?

If you'll update yourself on the pertinent issues before the next election, voting will be a snap. Remember, if you're not familiar with every candidate or every issue, you can skip that part. It's not necessary to vote for every office or measure to have your ballot counted.

Why not try teamwork for your next election? Divide the offices and issues among your prayer group, Bible study, or Sunday school class. Pick a date a week or two before the election. Have everyone bring their sample ballots and share information.

What can you do for your country? It may not seem like a big thing, but why not begin by making your vote count in the next election?

FOCUS POINT

You are important. *You* are vital—to our conservative movement and to our country that we love. Don't let us down!

INDEX

The typeface for the text of this book is *Palatino*. This type—best known as a contemporary *italic* typeface—was a post-World War II design crafted by the talented young German calligrapher Hermann Zapf. For inspiration, Zapf drew upon the writing legacy of a group of Italian Renaissance writing masters, in which the typeface's namesake, Giovanni Battista Palatino, was numbered. Giovanni Palatino's *Libro nuovo d'imparare a scrivera* was published in Rome in 1540 and became one of the most used, wide-ranging writing manuals of the sixteenth century. Zapf was an apt student of the European masters, and contemporary *Palatino* is one of his contributions to modern typography.

Substantive Editing:
Michael S. Hyatt

Copy Editing:
Cynthia Tripp

Cover Design:
Steve Diggs & Friends
Nashville, Tennessee

Page Composition:
Xerox Ventura Publisher
Printware 720 IQ Laser Printer

Printing and Binding:
Maple-Vail Printing Group
York, Pennsylvania

Dust Jacket Printing:
Strine Printing Company
York, Pennsylvania